Making Schools Different
Alternative Approaches to Educating Young People

Making Schools Different

Alternative Approaches to Educating Young People

Edited by Kitty te Riele

Los Angeles | London | New Delhi
Singapore | Washington DC

Editorial arrangement and Chapters 1 and 8 © Kitty te Riele
Chapter 2 © Laudan Aron
Chapter 3 © Frans Meijers
Chapter 4 © Meg Maguire
Chapter 5 © Helen Stokes & Johanna Wyn
Chapter 6 © Kitty te Riele & Frans Meijers
Chapter 7 © Kumari Beck & Wanda Cassidy
Chapter 9 © Linda Milbourne
Chapter 10 © Jann Eason & Linda Milbourne
Chapter 11 © Terri Seddon & Kathleen Ferguson
Chapter 12 © Stephen Crump
Chapter 13 © Marie Brennan, Eleanor Ramsay, Alison Mackinnon & Katherine Hodgetts
Chapter 14 © Kathleen Ferguson, Terri Seddon, Kylie Twyford, Stephen Crump & Katherine Hodgetts
Chapter 15 © Wanda Cassidy & Ann Chinnery

First published 2009

SAGE Publications Ltd
1 Oliver's Yard
55 City Road
London EC1Y 1SP

SAGE Publications Inc.
2455 Teller Road
Thousand Oaks, California 91320

SAGE Publications India Pvt Ltd
B 1/I 1 Mohan Cooperative Industrial Area
Mathura Road
New Delhi 110 044

SAGE Publications Asia-Pacific Pte Ltd
33 Pekin Street #02–01
Far East Square
Singapore 048763

Library of Congress Control Number: 2009926217

British Library Cataloguing in Publication data
A catalogue record for this book is available from the British
Library

ISBN 978–1-84787–529-7
ISBN 978–1-84787–530-3 (pbk)

Typeset by Dorwyn, Wells, Somerset
Printed in India by Replika Press Pvt Ltd
Printed on paper from sustainable resources

Contents

Foreword

'Most people, you know, they have been in school for so many years, they just want to get on with their lives now … not more writing and learning things that nobody cares about' (Wayne, quoted in Ball et al., 2000).

The non-participation of a small but entrenched minority of young people in education, training or employment in the period after the end of compulsory schooling remains an intractable and worrying problem in many Western societies – estimates of the size of this group range anywhere from 10–40 per cent of 14–25 year olds. Of course the 'problem' is construed in different ways by different constituencies, often with little recourse to the concerns of the young people themselves. It is an educational problem, particularly as these young people have typically had an unsatisfactory experience of compulsory schooling. Educational experiences have typically done little to contribute to a robust sense of self and have often instilled an enduring sense of inefficacy rather than resilience.

For Wayne, leaving school is not a stage in the continuity of learning – it is a break, a new beginning, an escape. An escape from the outlines of a 'totally pedagogised society' and the 'pedagogisation of life' in which learning is an activity that is conducted endlessly, 'in which the State is moving to ensure that there's no space or time which is not pedagogised' (Bernstein, 2001: 377). What Wayne's comment indicates is a different 'logic of practice' from that which underpins 'learning policy'. There is a mismatch between the logic and rhythms of policy and those of the lives of many young people.

As the papers in this collection demonstrate, non-participation and its concomitant alienations is also a social problem – non-participation places young people 'at risk'. And it is a political problem (in a variety of senses) – such young people are mostly unable to exercise the rights and responsibilities of citizenship, and fail to become subject to the increasingly hegemonic conception of the lifelong learner. The lifelong learner is a much over-burdened and over-determined social subject within current education policy and within some current versions of social theory. Lifelong learning indeed is subject to a constant stream of 'over blown policy statements' (Edwards and Nicoll, 2001: 104) which seek to position young people like Wayne, alongside others, as nothing less than a new kind of person, and within a new 'ethic of personhood'; 'an entire self must be completely made over as an enterprising individual' (McWilliam, 2002: 292).

But the real problem in all of this is policy itself and that the burden of policy is in fact focused in the wrong places, often on the young people themselves and their 'motivations' – a move which individualises and psychologises but which leaves policy itself and the institutional processes of schooling, or what te Riele calls the 'intractability of schooling', unaddressed. This book takes a different route and focuses on the need to 'do school differently' through innovations in learning, the use of time and place in different ways, and an engagement with complexity and diversity.

Stephen J. Ball
Karl Mannheim Professor of Sociology of Education
Institute of Education, University of London

About the authors

Editor

Kitty te Riele researches educational policy and practice for marginalized young people, including mainstream and alternative educational initiatives. She is interested in the ways schools can play a role both in marginalizing and in (re-)engaging young people. She is Senior Lecturer in Education in the Faculty of Arts and Social Sciences at the University of Technology Sydney (UTS), Australia where she teaches educational philosophy and professional ethics in Primary Education and in the doctoral research programme.

Contributors

Laudan Aron has over 20 years of professional experience conducting research and policy analysis on social welfare issues, including behavioural health and disability, child welfare and at-risk youth, education, employment and training, and homelessness and family violence. She has conducted studies for many US federal and state agencies and national foundations. She is currently the Director of Research at the National Alliance on Mental Illness (NAMI) where she oversees all of NAMI's research activities, including its ongoing report to the nation on public mental health service systems, *Grading the States*.

Kumari Beck is Assistant Professor in the Faculty of Education at Simon Fraser University in Canada. The primary site of her research is internationalization of higher education, in particular, the experiences of international students. Other research interests are located in the intersections of social education and the ethic of care, and include the exploration of social issues, inclusion, and relationships in advancing conceptions of social justice.

Marie Brennan is Professor of Education at the University of South Australia, where she recently completed a five-year term as Dean of Education. She currently teaches in curriculum studies and educational policy at graduate and undergraduate levels. A key researcher in the Centre for Studies in Literacy, Policy and Learning Cultures within the Hawke Research Institute, her research interests include: political sociology of school reform, especially curriculum; democratic and participatory forms of research, including action research; teacher education; and 'global south' issues. With Tom Popkewitz she co-edited the book *Foucault's Challenge: Discourse, Knowledge, and Power in Education*.

Wanda Cassidy is Associate Professor in the Faculty of Education at Simon Fraser University in Canada and Director of the Centre for Education, Law and Society, an endowed centre established to improve the legal literacy of children and youth through a programme of research, teaching, curriculum development and community-based initiatives. An important dimension of her research involves examining those values and beliefs that underpin the legal system and are instrumental in developing a just and caring society, including ethics of care, conceptions of diversity and inclusion, and notions of social responsibility.

Ann Chinnery is Assistant Professor in the Faculty of Education at Simon Fraser University in Canada. Her research addresses philosophical and ethical issues in teacher education, especially recent theoretical shifts in thinking about rights and responsibilities; the practical complexities of classroom dialogue in pluralist democracies; and preparing teachers for work in increasingly diverse classrooms.

Stephen Crump is Pro Vice-Chancellor and Director of the Central Coast Campuses and Professor in Education at the University of Newcastle. Stephen is chief investigator for an Australian Research Council project on interactive distance e-learning. He has (co-)authored 200 publications on educational policy, leadership, curriculum and organizational development. He led two major reports and an Australian Research Council (ARC) project on Vocational Education and Training for the New South Wales (NSW) and Commonwealth governments as well as a Taskforce into NSW matriculation certificate reforms.

Jann Eason is Principal of the Macleay Vocational College in Kempsey. This is an education and training facility for marginalized youth in a socially and economically depressed region of NSW. Macleay Vocational College is the brainchild of the local community. Macleay Vocational College was Jann's first appointment as a Principal in 2001 after 24 years experience as a secondary teacher. She was charged with designing and building this purpose-built education and training facility. In 2006 Jann was selected by Teaching Australia for the first round of the Leading Australia's Schools programme.

Kathleen Ferguson was Research Fellow on the Assessing New Learning Spaces project at the Faculty of Education, Monash University. She is now lecturing in the Socrates Programme in the Department of Sociology at the University of Warsaw, Poland. Kathleen has a PhD in Comparative Literature and Cultural Studies, and postdoctoral fellowship in Geography, University of Durham. Her research interests focus on embodied perception, cultural critique and 'hospitality industry' training.

Katherine Hodgetts is a postdoctoral research fellow in the Centre for Studies in Literacy, Policy and Learning Cultures at the University of South Australia. Her research applies discursive methods to the analysis of masculinity construction, educational gender equity and teachers' negotiation of gendered identities. Katherine's work on the ARC Linkage Project 'Pathways or cul de sacs? The causes, impact and implications of part-time senior secondary study' investigated students' negotiation of community, home, work and study commitments.

Alison Mackinnon (Emeritus Professor) has written widely on educational issues in both historical and contemporary contexts. She has an abiding interest in the ways in which class and gender shape educational opportunities. She is the author of several books, including *Love and Freedom: Professional Women and the Reshaping of Personal Life* (1997) which won a New South Wales Premier's Literary award. She is a Fellow of the Academy of the Social Sciences in Australia.

Meg Maguire is Professor of Sociology of Education at King's College London. Much of her work is concerned with social justice and policy in urban settings. She is lead editor of the *Journal of Education Policy*. Meg's latest books are *Becoming a Teacher: Issues in Secondary Teaching* (2007, 3rd edition, edited with Justin Dillon) and *Education, Globalization and New Times* (2007, edited with Stephen Ball and Ivor Goodson).

Frans Meijers was educated as a sociologist of education at the Catholic University of Nijmegen and earned his doctorate at the University of Leiden on vocational education policy 1945–75. After 20 years of working with the universities of Nijmegen, Amsterdam and Leiden, he set up his own company specializing in research and advice regarding 'career learning'. He is currently also part-time lecturer for 'Pedagogy of vocational development' at the Haagse Hogeschool (The Hague).

Linda Milbourne is programme director for Youth, Voluntary and Community Sector Studies in the Faculty of Lifelong Learning at Birkbeck College, London. Her research focuses on changing social and education policies, with a particular interest in community based services, inter-agency working and initiatives addressing social exclusion. Her current work explores concepts of active participation and community engagement, questioning whether recent youth schemes are generating new spaces for diverse groups of young people.

Eleanor Ramsay is Adjunct Professor in the Hawke Research Institute for Sustainable Societies at the University of South Australia. Her work traverses both educational research and public policy leadership, with a particular focus on gender matters. In the past she has worked as a teacher, a senior manager in public schooling authorities in two Australian states, a Pro Vice-Chancellor in a university, a trade union official and an educational activist.

Terri Seddon is Professor of Education at Monash University. Her research focuses on education (lifelong learning) and work. She is currently examining the way changes in work and society are diversifying learning spaces and what this means for continuity and change in educational work, with special attention to post-compulsory and adult education, training and in-place learning. She has strong links with European research and is actively engaged in local and transnational partnership work. Her books include *Context and Beyond* (1993); *Pay, Professionalism and Politics: Reforming Teachers? Reforming Education?* (1996) and *Beyond Nostalgia: Reshaping Australian Education* (2000, with Lawrie Angus).

Helen Stokes is a Research Fellow at the Youth Research Centre at the University of Melbourne. She has undertaken research and evaluation work in a number of education and youth areas in Australia including school to post-school transitions, school engagement (including the role of the arts), vocational education and training and early school leaving. International work has included a study of the situation of young people in Bhutan for the Youth Development Fund and the Ministry of Education in Bhutan.

Kylie Twyford works at the University of Newcastle as the Senior Research Associate on the Australian Research Council Linkage project, 'Interactive Distance eLearning for Isolated Communities: Opening our Eyes'. The project is investigating satellite delivered lessons provided to students in isolated homesteads and remote communities in Australia. Kylie previously worked for many years as a distance education teacher and manager in the vocational education and training sector (VET). Her area of research interest is in ICT in distance education and its influence on student motivation, participation and retention.

Johanna Wyn is Professor of Education and Director of the Youth Research Centre at the University of Melbourne. Her books include *Rethinking Youth* (1997, with Rob White), *Youth, Education and Risk: Facing the Future* (2001, with Peter Dwyer), *Youth and Society: Exploring the Social Dynamics of Youth* (2007, with Rob White) and *Youth Health and Welfare: The Cultural Politics of Education and Wellbeing* (2009).

Acknowledgements

As the editor, I would like to thank Jude Bowen at SAGE for supporting this book from our very first meeting, and all authors for their contributions to make the book a reality. Several chapters draw on (funded) research projects, which are listed below.

Chapter 7 The research was funded by a grant from the Social Sciences and Humanities Research Council of Canada. The research team included principal investigator, Dr Heesoon Bai, Dr Wanda Cassidy, co-investigator, and Dr Kumari Beck (then a doctoral student/research assistant), all from Simon Fraser University's Faculty of Education. Details of the study and further information can be obtained from the authors.

Chapter 8 Examples are drawn from two Australian research projects:
Project A: 'Alternative education for marginalised youth: negotiating risk and hope', funded through a grant by the University of Technology Sydney, carried out by the author, 2006–08.
Project B: 'Changing schools in changing times: stabilising and sustaining whole school change in communities experiencing adverse conditions', an ARC-Linkage project with the NSW Department of Education and Training, 2005–08. The project is led by Debra Hayes of the University of Sydney and team members include Narelle Carey, Ken Johnston, Ann King, Rani Lewis-Jones, Kristal Morris, Chris Murray, Ishbel Murray, Kerith Power, Dianne Roberts, Kitty te Riele and Margaret Wheeler.

Chapter 11 We want to thank the Australian Research Council (ARC), the European Union Commission, Victorian Department of Education and National Council for Vocational Education Research for funding the projects on which this chapter is based.

Chapter 12 The data reported on in this chapter comes from research (ARC LP0562535) led by the author as chief investigator and includes Brian Devlin (second chief investigator) and Amy Hutchinson, Charles Darwin University in the Northern Territory; Kylie Twyford, University of Newcastle, Australia, and Alan Anderson, Southern Cross University, NSW, Australia. The views expressed are my own and represent interim findings not yet endorsed by the industry partners.

Chapter 13 An earlier version of this paper was presented at the annual conference of the British Educational Research Association, Institute of Education London, September 2007. This paper is drawn from an Australian Research Council funded Linkage Project 'Pathways or cul-de-sacs? The causes, impact and implications of senior secondary part-time study', 2005–07 (LPO455760), conducted from 2005–07 with early work commencing in 2004. We are grateful to the ARC and peer reviewers for the project, to our research assistants over the project, Dr Lynette Arnold, Dr Katherine Hodgetts and Dr Kirrilly Thompson who have each come in at critical times to ensure that the work of the university chief investigators was able to be kept on track. Chief investigators on the project are: Professor Eleanor Ramsay, Professor Marie Brennan and Professor Alison Mackinnon from the University of South Australia, with partner investigators from the Department of Education and Children's Services: Wendy Engliss; Judith Lydeamore, Tanya Rogers, Bev Rogers (at different times); the Premier's Social Inclusion Unit, Dr Jan Patterson; and the state senior secondary curriculum authority, SSABSA: Dr Jan Keightley, then Dr Paul Kilvert. Our PhD student, Rochelle Woodley-Baker, has also been active in ensuring that gender issues and young people as agents in their own lives remained on the agenda.

Chapter 15 The research on Aboriginal education for this chapter was funded, in part, by the Department of Justice Canada, Youth Justice Fund. Principal investigator was Dr Wanda Cassidy, in association with Focus Foundation of British Columbia.

1 Educational innovation for young people

Kitty te Riele

This chapter sets the parameters for the kinds of educational innovation for young people that are needed – and that are expanded on in the remainder of the book. The chapter:

- discusses claims about the 'intractability' of schooling and supports an 'inside-out' approach to reform;

- outlines key societal changes that drive the need for doing school differently; and

- gives an overview of both the understanding of schooling and youth, and of the vision for innovation, that underpins this book.

Proposing that schooling should be done differently tends to run into two difficulties. First, people are quick to point out that educational practices are so entrenched that innovative attempts are doomed to fail. Secondly, if people allow that some reform is possible, controversy erupts about what that reform should look like. In this introductory chapter for the book, I start with the first difficulty, analysing persistent default practices and suggestions for enabling change from the inside out. Next I turn to the second difficulty, by exploring the kind of social changes I consider especially pertinent to young people and outlining the implications of these changes and the vision for innovation that underpin this book.

The intractability of schooling

Studies of education can be broadly grouped on two sides: those that analyse what is wrong with education and those that provide solutions. The former range from doomsday newspaper reports blaming schools for all that is wrong with society to careful sociological attempts to outline why (in one famous title) schooling cannot compensate for society (Bernstein, 1977). The latter include not only myriad practical handbooks with handy hints for teachers but also results of often large-scale research on what contributes to school improvement. This book belongs in neither camp. It recognizes the inherent contradiction pointed out by Grace:

> between analyses which suggest growing or insipient crisis and reports which document and exemplify school reform and progress. This can be confusing to students and teachers in the urban education field, who assume that once the causes of the crisis have been identified and once examples of good educational practice have been closely studied there will be some sustained and linear improvement in urban education systems. (1994: 46)

Grace's suggestion for an approach built on complex hope, drawing on localized examples of good practice in the face of challenging circumstances, underpins this book. The premise for the book is not to ignore difficult circumstances, but to take the analysis of these only as a starting point, rather than as the end (see Shade, 2006).

This means it is necessary to take seriously the critique that schooling is intractable, that is, it resists any attempts to change, influence or manipulate it in a significant way. Tyack and Cuban (1995: 86) explain that established traditions of schooling 'come to be understood by educators, students and the public as necessary features of a "real school" […]. They become just the way schools are'. For example, a now classic study from the USA was struck by the sameness of schooling across the 13 primary, 12 junior high and 12 senior high schools it studied. Observations in classrooms provided nine patterns of teaching and learning that were largely common across schools, despite their external differences (Goodlad, 1984: 123–4):

1. Dominance of whole-class teaching, by one teacher for 20–30 students.
2. Students work and achieve mostly alone, there is little collaboration.
3. The teacher is the central figure who makes almost all decisions.
4. The teacher is dominant in the conduct of instruction – students rarely learn from one another.
5. There is paucity of praise and correction by the teacher.
6. Little variety in classroom activities – listening to the teacher, writing answers to questions, and taking tests and quizzes.
7. Variety is greatest in lower grades (early/mid primary) and least in secondary school.
8. Many students were nevertheless quite happy with schooling.
9. Students often did not understand or have time to finish what their teacher wanted them to do.

Although this study was conducted in the early 1980s, many of these patterns still strike true. A recent Australian study conducted classroom observations in the junior classes of four disadvantaged high schools and noted that patterns of inter-action between students and teachers were surprisingly similar (Johnston and Hayes, 2008: 114). They point to five key features which are rephrased here to highlight the similarities with several of Goodlad's patterns above.

1. Little variety in classroom activities – listening to the teacher, answering questions, and completing worksheets or other tasks (usually individually, occasionally in groups).
2. Limited demands in terms of literacy.
3. Limited intellectual demands (mostly factual and procedural).
4. The teacher is dominant in instruction and asking basic questions – students rarely engage in open discussion with each other or the teacher.
5. The teacher makes the decisions – students had no choice in what, how or when to learn.

The focus of the studies by Goodlad (1984) and Johnston and Hayes (2008) was different, they were conducted in different countries and more than 20 years apart. Nevertheless, the central role of the teacher, the repetitiveness of activities and the low level of intellectual engagement characterize classrooms in both stud-ies. This approach remains dominant:

> not because it has been shown to be a particularly good way to educate human beings, but because it works well in rooms of 600 square feet that are filled with twenty-five young people, more than two-thirds of whom, if given a choice, are likely to choose to be somewhere else. (Fenstermacher and Soltis, 1998: 22)

The pessimism expressed in phrases such as the persistent 'grammar of schooling' (Tyack and Cuban, 1995: 85) and the 'widespread and resilient logic of practice' (Johnston and Hayes, 2008: 110) is understandable in the light of such evidence.

What does this mean? We can either accept the default, even though few edu-cators would consider it optimal, or we can continue to look for and find ways to do schooling differently – and better. As stated above, this book agrees with Shade (2006: 212) in perceiving that 'a realistic appraisal of current conditions is a start-ing and not a terminal point' – and thus chooses the second option.

Inside-out reform

At times, radical change is advocated as the way forward. Goodlad (1984: 249) suggests that 'mere refinement of conventional practice is not sufficient'. Going further, Elmore (2006: n.p.) argues that the traditional school culture 'has been defeating people who try to change it for decades. You don't change a culture like this – you replace it!'

This book does not support such dramatic reform. As Tyack and Cuban (1995) so convincingly demonstrate, this kind of reform rarely lasts – even when it is based on good ideas in the first place. They analyse historical examples of large-scale innovations adopted by school districts and other bureaucracies, supported by academics or education associations, or pushed by corporations – and are gloomy about the outcomes:

> For over a century, ambitious reformers have promised to create sleek, efficient school machines 'light years' ahead of the fusty schools of their times. But in practice their reforms have often resembled shooting stars that spurted across the pedagogical heavens, leaving a meteoric trail in the media but burning up and disappearing in the everyday atmosphere of the schools. (Tyack and Cuban, 1995: 111)

A major reason for the long-term (and sometimes even short-term) failure of top-down reforms are the translations that happen along the way. Bernstein (2000) points to three key sites in the life of a reform strategy. The strategy begins in a site of production, whether it is a scholarly site (such as the work by Elmore, 2006) or a for-profit think tank (see examples in Tyack and Cuban, 1995). This is where the research and development work takes place to construct ideas for reform. The second site consists of educational bureaucracies (government districts and departments or non-government foundations or associations) that selectively reinterpret these ideas and translate them into practical guidelines and policy documents. A further translation occurs as these documents enter schools and classrooms, where staff attempt to apply, adapt or resist the officially endorsed reform strategy. The translations and reinterpretations that happen along the way inevitably alter the strategy – usually back towards the default grammar of schooling. Elmore's (2006) suggestion about education reform that 'you take [the current culture] out and put something else in its place' is not only patronizing but unrealistic and naive about the complexities of the relations of schooling.

However, the phenomenon of reform (re-)translation does not mean that it is impossible to improve education, to change the default grammar so as to do schooling differently. Schools have diverse, ambiguous and contradictory purposes and effects. In a context of the broad similarities pointed out above, individual teachers and schools nevertheless continue to demonstrate different approaches (for example, Johnston and Hayes, 2008: 119) in the face of restrictions posed by bureaucratic requirements and cultural expectations. Despite their critical analysis of the history of school reform in the USA, Tyack and Cuban remain cautiously optimistic: 'We do not expect some magical Phoenix to arise from the "ashes" of the current system. We do not believe in educational Phoenixes and do not think that the system is in ashes' (1995: 134).

While acknowledging cultural, structural and systemic constraints, this book supports a perspective on how to change schooling that starts with the current system, so that 'the actual [is] reinterpreted and reconstructed in the light of the possible' (Alexander, 1990, in Russell, 1999: 103). Default practices can be challenged because they remain in place at least partly due to 'unexamined institutional habits and widespread cultural beliefs' (Tyack and Cuban, 1995: 88) so that teachers are 'restrained by the power of existing regularities [and do not] attempt to explore other possibilities' (Goodlad, 1984: 249). This book aims to provide teachers and youth workers first and foremost, but also scholars and policy-makers, with tools for examining such taken-for-granted habits and beliefs, thus enabling them to explore options for doing schooling differently.

Most importantly, this means working with and supporting practitioners – to try out new ideas as well as to continue with the good work individual teachers and schools are already doing. Such a 'chalk face' approach reinvigorates hope for social and educational change. Understanding as well as action must start within local and specific situations. As Crump (1995: 212) explained 'local struggles are an expression of what is occurring, or possible, at regional, state, national and even international levels'. Tyack and Cuban (1995: 133, 135) outline what this means for school reform:

> Rather than starting from scratch in reinventing schools, it makes most sense to us to graft thoughtful reforms onto what is healthy in the present system. Schooling is being reinvented all the time, but not necessarily in ways envisaged in macro planning. Good teachers reinvent the world every day for the children in their classes. [...] Better schooling will result in the future – as it has in the past and does now – chiefly from the steady reflective efforts of the practitioners who work in schools.

This book therefore proposes to 'focus on ways to improve instruction from the inside out rather than the top down' (Tyack and Cuban, 1995: 134). This places much more emphasis on the active involvement of teachers to draw on resources for innovation (provided by themselves as well as scholars, corporations and policy) and adapt these flexibly to their own circumstances and local knowledge.

Societal changes

This book appreciates the diversification of recognized learning sites and schools which have attempted to respond constructively to social, economic and technological changes to better cater for a diversity of young people by changing the experience of schooling. The book has its origin in both educational research and practices that ask questions and explore contradictions within established and changing patterns of educational institutions and of young people's lives. It aims to provide some answers about how schooling can be done differently to suit several major societal changes.

First, social and political change since the mid-1980s has seen a shift from community to more individual orientations. This trend towards individualization has also affected the discursive construction of young people's experiences. It has been suggested that in contemporary 'late-modern' society 'choice biographies' have replaced the 'normal biographies' of the industrial world (Beck, 1992). Choice biography may be interpreted positively as providing agency or more negatively as forcing people to make decisions even if their options are limited. Beck points to the coercive aspect of choice – people inevitably *must* construct a great proportion of their biography personally: 'Even when the word "decisions" is too grandiose, because neither consciousness nor alternatives are present, the individual will have to "pay for" the consequences of decisions not taken' (Beck, 1992: 135). A tension between freedom and coercion is inherent in choice biographies. In either case, it contributes to an impression of personal responsibility not only for life experiences, but also for constructing a viable personal identity.

A second major change has been the rise of the knowledge society. Across the industrialized world, economic prosperity has become increasingly reliant on knowledge or information (Thurow, 1999). This has had a major impact on education and training for young people. National policies to increase participation in education together with the collapse of the youth labour market have put pressure on young people to remain in or return to education. The observation by Furlong and Cartmel (1997: 17) in the UK that this 'has produced an army of reluctant conscripts to post-compulsory education' has international resonance. Recent policy moves to extend the compulsory age for school attendance (for example, to 16 in the state of New South Wales, Australia, and to 17 in the UK, see Chapter 4 in this volume) further reinforce this. Engaging a much broader range of young people in extended schooling requires renewed consideration of pedagogical approaches.

Finally, complexity in young people's lives has implications for education, especially in terms of its timing and location. While schooling continues to take up a large part of young lives, there is increasing recognition that this sits alongside their work, sport, music, peer and family commitments. Spierings suggests the metaphor of a mosaic: 'Young people, both as teenagers and as young adults, are required to put all the pieces into place and to find the answers to life's jigsaw using their own devices' (1999: 7). Although the mosaic has various components, work and education are especially important. For example, in Australia about half of young people combine full-time schooling with part-time study (Vickers et al., 2003). One of the key features identified by the Organisation for Economic Co-operation and Development (OECD) (in AIG/DSF, 2007: 19) as contributing to a successful transition from education to work for young people is 'workplace experience combined with education'. Nevertheless, schools in general are not yet used to making constructive use of the work experience students gain in their part-time jobs, nor to giving genuine recognition for the competing demands on young people's time and energy.

Implications and vision

The three societal changes above have some specific implications for the approach taken in this book. First, both schooling and young people are conceptualized broadly. Schooling here includes a range of formal, credentialed education and training options for young people – including vocational and general, part-time and re-entry, and in traditional as well as alternative settings.

While youth may be defined as the phase of life between childhood and adulthood, individuals negotiate the transition to adulthood at different speeds and at different ages. Markers of adulthood are increasingly unclear, as young people move between work and education, and between living independently and with their parents. At the same time traditional teenage lifestyles, in relation to patterns of consumption and dress, are increasingly adopted by children under the age of 12. It is therefore impossible to give definite ages when youth begins and ends, although it is likely to continue to extend, at the upper as well as the lower end. As a rough guide, most chapters in this book refer to young people aged between 15 and 25, but some examples will include younger or older students.

The final implication is that the book focuses especially on those young people currently served least well by various forms of schooling. The intention is not to stereotype marginalized young people. As Raywid (1994) argues, marginalized students are quite similar to the rest of the student population. For example Dwyer (1996) estimated that on top of the quarter or so of actual early school leavers in Australia, another quarter of students in senior high school would prefer to leave if they could. In Holdsworth's (2004: 4) portrayal, these young people 'sit in classrooms, passively cooperating, even responding positively, but waiting for the bell'. Although they do not actively rebel against school, they would rather do it differently. However, as Raywid (1994: 27) further suggests, marginalized students 'are just more dependent on a good education'. The argument underpinning this book is that reforms that make schooling work better for marginalized students can provide insights to improve schooling for most students in regular schools as well.

The focus on innovation and on catering better for marginalized youth in this book means many chapters draw on examples from non-traditional schools. For this reason, the next chapter outlines a broad concept of alternative education, why it is needed and how it may be understood.

Following Chapter 2, the book is organized around three themes: identity, pedagogy, and place and time. Each theme not only relates to the societal changes outlined above, but also represents a dimension of education and training that provides opportunities for catering better for a diversity of young people by 'doing school differently'.

The first theme highlights changes in youth identity and ways in which schooling can respond and contribute constructively to these identities. Chapters 3, 4 and 5 provide scholarly views, while Chapter 6 incorporates two practical case studies that demonstrate how schooling may be done differently in response to the issues raised about identity.

The second theme addresses how teaching can be done differently to engage all young people, including the most marginalized. Chapters 7, 8 and 9 present academic perspectives, again followed by a chapter (10) that applies these ideas in two case studies.

The third theme demonstrates how the stereotypical image of school as separate from the world (Ferguson and Seddon, 2007) can be challenged to organize schooling in different places and/or at different times to better suit a diverse range of young people. Chapters 11, 12 and 13 offer research-based discussions, with Chapter 14 including three further practical case studies. The book is concluded by Chapter 15 which considers all three themes through an indigenous education vision.

The book brings together important new perspectives on the opportunities provided by the changed experience of youth in current economic and social contexts. It offers both practitioners and researchers insights into questions about how to think differently about education for young people as well as reflections on projects and programmes that have attempted to put such thoughts into practice. The suggestions provided in the chapters tackle some of the real difficulties many young people, educational institutions and policy-makers face.

Providing ideas and practical examples for doing school differently, this book does not advocate simplistic hope but rather contributes to a 'continuing source of optimism of the will' (Grace, 1994: 56) in education. The research and cases presented can be used imaginatively by educational practitioners, administrators and researchers to improve education for all young people. I encourage you to use it in the spirit of Max Lerner's vision (Lagemann, 1992: 201) of being neither an optimist nor a pessimist but a possibilist:

A possibilist would be able to approach educational problems with an eagerness to explore new ideas and practices, but without a willingness to be carried away by inflated expectations or promises. Knowing that panaceas abound in education and that prudence is rare, a possibilist would profoundly understand the vital importance of education and the perpetually imperfect nature of the endeavour. Most of all, perhaps, a possibilist would recognise the degree to which education is enmeshed in the historic problems and the contemporary and future prospects of the society of which it is a part.

Discussion questions

1. Do the patterns of classroom interaction outlined by Goodlad (1984) and Johnston and Hayes (2008) strike true? How might those patterns be changed?
2. How will society continue to change over the next few decades and what implications does that have for schooling and for young people?

Further reading

Ball, S., Goodson, I. and Maguire, M. (2007) *Education, Globalisation and New Times.* London: Routledge.

Grace, G. (1994) 'Urban education and the culture of contentment: the politics, culture, and economics of inner-city schooling', in N. Stromquist (ed.), *Education in Urban Areas: Cross-national Dimensions.* Westport, CT: Praeger. pp. 45–59.

Tyack, D. and Cuban, L. (1995) *Tinkering toward Utopia: A Century of Public School Reform.* Cambridge, MA: Harvard University Press.

World Bank (2005) *Expanding Opportunities and Building Competencies for Young People: A New Agenda for Secondary Education.* Washington, DC: World Bank.

Websites

Australian National Schools Network: http://www.ansn.edu.au/

Coalition of Essential Schools: http://www.essentialschools.org/pub/ces_docs/about/about.html

2 Alternative schooling in the USA

Laudan Aron

This chapter outlines a broad concept of alternative education, why it is needed and how it may be understood. The chapter:

- provides an overview of the need for alternative schooling in the USA;
- describes what is meant by the term 'alternative schools' and reviews several proposed typologies of such schools; and
- examines the characteristics of high-quality programmes and the outcomes that alternative schools should be able to demonstrate.

Like many other countries, the USA has a long history of alternative schooling and education system reform. These efforts have taken on a sense of urgency for at least the past quarter century. We have gone from being 'a nation at risk', the title of a high-profile 1983 publication sounding alarms about the quality of the nation's schools (National Commission on Excellence in Education, 1983), to being in the midst of what some are calling a 'quiet crisis' in education (Smith, 2004). This crisis includes a major dropout problem and a lesser known but equally important 'skills gap'.

In response, states and school districts across the country have been pushing for higher academic standards, more rigorous graduation requirements and greater accountability. In the USA, education is primarily the responsibility of state and local governments, but through the legislative process the federal government supports state activities. At the federal level, legislation known as the No Child Left Behind Act has attempted to strengthen the nation's schools through a system of state standards, new tests and a national accountability system, including a targeted effort to help low-performing schools and students. One unfortunate consequence of this movement towards greater accountability, high-stakes testing and new zero-tolerance disciplinary policies is that some low-performing students are not just dropping out of schools but may be getting pushed out.

This 'quiet crisis' has clear implications for the nation as a whole. Ninety per cent of the fastest growing jobs in the knowledge economy require some post-secondary education (US Government Accountability Office, 2007), but as the US Chamber of Commerce, representing more than 3 million businesses across the country, observes:

> Despite decades of reform efforts and many trillions of dollars in public investment, US schools are not equipping our children with the skills and knowledge they – and the nation – so badly need. It has been nearly a quarter century since the seminal report *A Nation at Risk* was issued in 1983. Since that time, a knowledge-based economy has emerged, the Internet has reshaped commerce and communication, exemplars of creative commerce like Microsoft, eBay, and Southwest Airlines have revolutionized the way we live, and the global economy has undergone wrenching change. Throughout that period, education spending has steadily increased and rafts of well-intentioned school reforms have come and gone. But student achievement has remained stagnant, and our K–12 schools have stayed remarkably unchanged – preserving, as if in amber, the routines, culture, and operations of an obsolete 1930s manufacturing plant. (Institute for a Competitive Workforce, 2008)

Estimates drawing on unpublished data from the Bureau of Labor Statistics, show that in 2003 there were 1.1 million youth aged 16 to 19 who did not have a high school diploma (or an alternative credential known as the General Educational Development test, or GED) and were not enrolled in school; another 2.4 million youth age 20 to 24 were in the same situation for a grand total of 3.5 million youth (Barton, 2005).

While the failure of 'traditional' schools for many young people is clear, the 'alternatives' we have in place are too few and most are of unknown quality. There is no precise accounting of the number or types of alternative schools or programmes in the USA. Available estimates suggest that there are over 20,000 alternative schools and programmes currently in operation, most designed to reach students at risk of school failure, not those who are out of school (Lange and Sletten, 2002). The number of full-time, federally funded education, employment and national service programmes available to teenaged high school dropouts is estimated at 100,000 (based on an estimated total of 300,000 opportunities for the 2.4 million low-income 16- to 24-year-olds who left school without a diploma or received a diploma but could not find a job) (Barton, 2005). Whatever the exact numbers, when it comes to alternative education for vulnerable youth, demand is far outpacing supply.

High-quality, alternative pathways to educational and vocational success are needed for children and youth of all ages. In thinking about alternative education, it is important to remember that young people do not disconnect from traditional developmental pathways (or high schools for that matter) because of the failure of any one system. Likewise, *reconnecting* youth requires collaboration and coordination among multiple youth-serving systems. In addition to school and youth employment and training programmes, these systems include child protection and juvenile justice, and a variety of health and social welfare agencies (such as mental health and substance abuse treatment programmes, crisis intervention centres, and runaway and homeless youth shelters). Finally, one should acknowledge that communities, neighbourhoods, families, adult mentors and peers can also have a major influence on the developmental trajectories of children and youth.

What do we mean by 'alternative education'?

The term 'alternative education' in its broadest sense covers all educational activities that fall outside the *traditional* K–12 school system (including home schooling, GED preparation programmes, special programmes for gifted children, charter schools). However, the term is often used to describe programmes serving vulnerable youth who are either at risk of dropping out or are no longer in traditional schools. Ironically, because they are often associated with students who were unsuccessful in the past, many alternative schools are thought to be of much poorer quality than the traditional K–12 school system, and yet because they are challenged to motivate and educate disengaged students many alternative education programmes are known for their innovation and creativity.

The Common Core of Data, the US Department of Education's primary database on public elementary and secondary education, defines an alternative education school as 'a public elementary/secondary school that addresses needs of students that typically cannot be met in a regular school, provides nontraditional education, serves as an adjunct to a regular school, or falls outside the categories of regular, special education or vocational education' (US NCES, 2002: 14, table 2).

A definitive typology of the many types of alternative education schools and programmes that fall within this rather broad definition has yet to be developed and accepted by the field. Many dimensions of interest that could be used to develop a typology of alternative schools and programmes have been identified (Aron and Zweig, 2003). In the early 1990s, Mary Anne Raywid (1994: 26–31) proposed a typology based on a programme's goals as their distinguishing characteristic. Despite being quite old, Raywid's typology is still widely used, in part because it captures such a full continuum of existing programme types:

- Type I schools 'offer full-time, multiyear, education options for students of all kinds, including those needing more individualization, those seeking an innovative or challenging curriculum, or dropouts wishing to earn their diplomas. A full instructional program offers students the credits needed for graduation. Students choose to attend. [...] Models range from schools-within-schools to magnet schools, charter schools, schools without walls, experiential schools, career-focused and job-based schools, dropout-recovery programs, after-hours schools, and schools in atypical settings like shopping malls and museums' (ibid.).

- Type II schools' distinguishing 'characteristic is discipline, which aims to segregate, contain, and reform disruptive students. Students typically do not choose to attend, but are sent to the school for specified time periods or until behavior requirements are met. Since placement is short-term, the curriculum is limited to a few basic, required courses or is entirely supplied by the "home school" as a list of assignments. Familiar models include last-chance schools and in-school suspension' (ibid.).

- Type III programs 'provide short-term but therapeutic settings for students with social and emotional problems that create academic and behavioral barriers to learning. Although Type III programs target specific populations – offering counselling, access to social services, and academic remediation – students can choose not to participate' (ibid.).

The first group includes many of the original alternative education programmes developed for at-risk youth and are often referred to as 'popular innovations' or 'true educational alternatives'. Programmes for high school dropouts (or potential dropouts) sponsored by school districts would fit into this category, along with newer programmes for students unable to pass standardized tests (Krentz et al., 2005). The other two types are more correctional in focus, one being primarily disciplinary ('last chance' or 'soft jail' programmes) and the other therapeutic ('treatment' programmes). Most of these operate separately from regular schools, although they can be sponsored by school districts.

Preliminary research by Raywid and others suggests that the first group of programmes – the true educational alternatives – are the most successful, while alternative discipline programmes are much less likely to lead to substantial student gains. Rigorous evaluation studies are still needed, but anecdotal evidence suggests that outcomes for therapeutic programmes are more mixed, with students often making progress while enrolled but regressing when they return to a more traditional school.

It should also be noted that as more programmes develop a mix of strategies and approaches, often intended to meet multiple needs, the distinctions between Raywid's groupings can blur. So for example, Type I and Type II schools are increasingly likely to offer clinical counselling (a Type III characteristic).

Another promising typology, proposed by Melissa Roderick, of the University of Chicago, puts students' educational needs at front and centre. Rather than focusing on a student's demographic characteristic (or 'risk factor') or even a programme characteristic, this typology focuses on the educational challenges students present (Aron and Zweig, 2003: 28). Roderick has identified several distinct groups:

- Students who have fallen 'off track' because they have got into trouble and need short-term systems of recovery to route them back into high schools. The goal of getting them back into regular high schools is both appropriate and realistic for this group.

- Students who have prematurely transitioned to adulthood either because they are (about to become) parents, or have home situations that do not allow them to attend school regularly (for example, immigrant children taking care of siblings while their parents work, those coming out of the juvenile justice system with many demands on their time).

- Students who have fallen substantially off track educationally, but are older and are returning to obtain the credits they need to transition into community colleges (or other programmes) very rapidly. These include, for example, older individuals who are just a few credits away from graduation (many of whom dropped out at age 16 or 17), or are transitioning out of the jail system, or have had a pregnancy and are now ready to complete their secondary schooling. Roderick notes that these students are currently populating most alternative education programmes in large urban areas – they are a very diverse group and tend to be well served by the existing alternative school system.

- The final group consists of students who have fallen substantially behind educationally – they have significant problems, very low reading levels and are often way over age for grade. Many of these children have been retained repeatedly and a number of them have come out of special education. They include 17- or 18-year-olds with third and fourth grade reading levels who have never graduated from eighth grade (or who have gone to high school for a few years but have never actually accumulated any credits). This is a very large group of youth, and most school systems do not have any programmes that can meet their needs.

Roderick argues that by targeting a particular demographic or 'problem' group, such as pregnant/parenting teens, programmes may be setting themselves up for failure if the students in a single programme encompass too much educational diversity. As a group, pregnant/parenting teens may include students who are two credits away from graduation, others who are wards of child welfare agencies and who have multiple problems such as being far over age for grade, and yet others who have significant behavioural problems and may be weaving in and out of the juvenile justice system. No single school or programme can be expected to handle such a wide array of educational and other needs.

What characterizes high-quality alternative education programmes?

Research on what works and for whom in alternative education is still evolving. There are few scientifically based, rigorous evaluations establishing which programme components lead to various positive outcomes for different subgroups of youth. The newness of the field means that researchers and policy-makers are still examining the characteristics of promising programmes, but lists of these characteristics are starting to converge and point to the variables that should be measured and monitored as more rigorous evaluations are designed and conducted. These characteristics include the following (drawn from a summary reported in Aron, 2006):

- Academic instruction. Successful programmes have a clear focus on academic learning that combines high academic standards with engaging and creative instruction and a culture of high expectations for all students. Learning must be relevant and applicable to life outside school and to future learning and work opportunities. Applied learning is an important component of the academic programme. This is often where employers can play important roles as partners. The curricula address the education and career interests of the students. The curricula are academically rigorous and tied to state standards and accountability systems. The students, staff and parents know and share the learning goals. Students have personalized learning plans and set learning goals based on their individual plans. There are opportunities for youth to catch up and accelerate knowledge and skills. A mixture of instructional approaches is available to help youth achieve academic objectives.

- Instructional staff. Instructors in successful alternative programmes choose to be part of the programme, routinely employ positive discipline techniques and establish rapport with students and peers. They have high expectations of the youth, are certified in their academic content area and are creative in their classrooms. They have a role in governing the school and designing the programme and curriculum.

- Professional development. Successful alternative education programmes provide instructors with ongoing professional development activities that help them maintain an academic focus, enhance teaching strategies and develop alternative instructional methods. Staff development involves teacher input, work with colleagues and opportunities to visit and observe teaching in other settings.

- Size. Many alternative education programmes are small with a low teacher/student ratio and have small classes that encourage caring relationships between youth and adults.

- Facility. Effective alternative learning programmes are in clean and well-maintained buildings (not necessarily a traditional school building) that are attractive and inviting and that foster emotional well-being, a sense of pride, and safety. In some instances, the programmes are located away from other high schools in 'neutral' territory. Most are close to public transportation.

- Relationships/building a sense of community. Successful alternative education programmes link to a wide variety of community organizations (cultural, social service, educational, and so on) and the business community to provide assistance and opportunities for participants. Through partnerships with the business community, alternative education providers are able to provide their students with job shadowing and internship opportunities, guest speakers and company tours, and receive valuable input into their curriculum and project development. Connections with community organizations can provide health care, mental health services, cultural and recreational opportunities for youth in their schools.

- Leadership, governance, administration and oversight. Many studies highlight the need for administrative and bureaucratic autonomy and operational flexibility. Administrators, teachers, support services staff, students and parents should be involved in the different aspects of the programme. This autonomy builds trust and loyalty among the staff. A successful alternative education programme has a strong, engaged, continuous and competent leadership, preferably with a teacher/director administering the programme.

- Student supports. Successful alternative education programmes support their students through flexible individualized programming with high expectations and clear rules of behaviour. They provide opportunities for youth to participate and have a voice in school matters. Structure, curricula and supportive services are designed with both the educational and social needs of the student in mind. Many schools do daily follow-up with all students who are absent or tardy and develop reward systems to promote attendance and academic achievement. Programmes are both highly structured and extremely flexible. Rules for the school, which the students help create, are few, simple and consistently enforced. There are processes in place that assist students in transitioning from school to work and from high school to post-high school training.

- Other contributing factors include clearly identified goals; the integration of research into practice in areas such as assessment, curriculum and teacher training; the integration of special education services and English Language Learning (ELL); and stable and diverse funding.

An interesting aspect of this list is how universal and appealing it is. These are qualities that would seem to benefit *any* educational programme, not just 'alternative' ones. This supports the idea that while current approaches to alternative education may be defined by and understood as being 'different' from mainstream educational options, one future vision is that communities have an array of high-quality educational options that all share many of these desirable characteristics.

What should alternative education programmes accomplish?

Currently there are few rigorous studies that examine the effectiveness of alternative education programmes in terms of student outcomes. Much more research is needed in this area, especially given that performance measures used by mainstream schools may not be appropriate for some alternative schools or programmes.

Work has advanced on what types of outcome measures *should* be targeted and monitored. Alternative education programmes are first and foremost *educational* programmes, so they need to focus on preparing students academically while also meeting the additional needs of their students. Evaluations of the programmes should include a variety of educational and other outcomes for participants.

Aron and Zweig (2003) have already noted the importance of developing accountability systems as well as better data collection and analysis that would support such systems. Part of the challenge involves figuring out 'how to introduce high academic standards in alternative education systems without sacrificing the elements that make alternative programmes successful, and without compromising the integrity of the high standards' (NGA Center for Best Practices, 2001: 1). Recommendations designed to strengthen the adoption of high standards by alternative education programmes include:

- improving 'early warning systems' to identify lower-performing students;
- collecting and analysing student-level data;
- developing enhanced GED programmes;
- developing data-driven accountability measures for alternative education programmes;
- strengthening links between traditional and non-traditional education systems;
- investing resources to support the transition to high academic standards and beyond; and

- supporting longer-term alternative education programmes.

Along with high standards should come adequate and reliable funding. Adopting a single high standard, even a voluntary standard, would help the field identify and promote those high-quality alternatives that deserve more support and replication across communities, and eliminate those low-performing ones that are not serving young people well. It would also go a long way towards increasing the legitimacy of alternative offerings, demonstrating the feasibility (and desirability) of offering multiple high-quality options and even integrating the traditional and alternative ends of the educational continuum. Ironically, these two ends are not so far apart. As Raywid observed in 1994 and which is still true today:

> Amid all the current talk of school restructuring, alternatives are the clearest example we have of what a restructured school might look like. They represent our most definitive departure from the programmatic, organizational and behavioral regularities that inhibit school reform. Moreover, many of the reforms currently pursued in traditional schools – downsizing the high school, pursuing a focus or theme, students and teacher choice, making the school a community, empowering staff, active learner engagement, authentic assessment – are practices that alternative schools pioneered. (1994: 26)

Discussion questions

1. What can and should local communities do to develop a portfolio of high-quality schooling options that best matches the educational needs of young people? How might these portfolios differ from one community to another, or in one community over time?
2. What can and should be done at the local, regional and national levels to raise the profile of alternative schools and the widespread need for such schools? What can traditional schools learn from high-quality alternative schools and vice versa?
3. Can we dispense with the labels 'traditional' and 'alternative' when it comes to schools? What exactly are these terms meant to reflect, and are there other, better, terms that capture what we usually mean when we talk about a traditional or alternative school?

Further reading

Dignity in Schools Campaign (2007) *Alternative Schools and Pushout: Research and Advocacy Guide*. Retrieved 13 September 2008 from http://www.nesri.org/

fact_sheets_pubs/DSC_Alternartive_Schools_Guide.pdf

Education Evolving (2008) *The Other Half of the Strategy: Following Up on System Reform by Innovating with School and Schooling.* Saint Paul, MN: Education Evolving. Retrieved 13 September 2008 from http://www.educationevolving.org/pdf/Innovatingwithschooling.pdf

Wehling. B. (ed.) (2007) *Building a 21st Century US Education System.* Washington, DC: National Commission on Teaching and America's Future (NCTAF). Retrieved 13 September 2008 from http://www.nctaf.org/resources/research_and_reports/nctaf_research_reports/documents/Bldg21stCenturyUSEducationSystem_final.pdf

3 The need for dialogue in vocational education

Frans Meijers

This chapter stresses the need for career learning in vocational education. The chapter will:

- explain how the individualization of society and the rise of a service economy ask for self-directed learning with regard to careers;
- present empirical evidence that makes clear that a strong career-learning environment is a dialogical environment; and
- provide practical examples drawn from research.

More than 2,000 years ago, the Roman philosopher Seneca succinctly formulated the importance of school in the sentence '*Non scolae sed vitae discimus*' (Not for school, but for life, do we learn). Even so, most students in the Dutch educational system have little idea at the beginning of their study (but also often long after that) exactly why they are there.

If one asked them, most would say that they are investing in their future. However, if one asks further as to what that future may hold, the silence is deafening. Most young people invest 'blindly' in their future, mainly because their environment – correctly – made clear to them that a diploma is important. As early as 1961, Schelsky (1961: 14) remarked that education had become 'the primary, determining, and almost unique social allocation authority for status, employment opportunities, and survival for an individual'. Parents respond to the increasing social meritocracy by keeping their children in school longer, or by pressuring them to remain in school as long as possible. Primary vocational education is the only place where these dynamics do not exist; children are 'sent' to this form of education by their score on national mathematical and verbal achievement tests, which are administered at the end of primary school.[1] This mostly

involves children from families with little cultural, scholastic and economic capital, in which little value is attached to investing in education. However, in
vocational education, students have developed hardly any career perspectives at
all, a concern that applies to their peers in the rest of the secondary educational
system as well (Ester et al., 2003; Meijers et al., 2006).

The consequence of this is that most young people – whether they attend primary
vocational education or university – employ a survival strategy. This strategy is
described by Holt on the basis of his observations as a high school teacher:

> It has become clear [to me] over the [last] year that these children see school almost
> entirely in terms of the day-to-day and hour-to-hour tasks that we impose on them.
> [...] School feels like this to children: it is a place where they make you go and where
> they tell you to do things and where they try to make your life unpleasant if you don't
> do them right. For children, the central business of school is not learning, whatever
> this vague word means; it is getting these tasks done, or at least out of the way, with a
> minimum of effort and unpleasantness. Each task is an end in itself. The children
> don't care how they dispose of it. If they can get it out of the way by doing it, they'll
> do it; if experience has taught them that this does not work very well, they will turn
> to other means, illegitimate means, that wholly defeat whatever purpose the task-giver
> may have had in mind. (1995: 47)

The lack of a clear future in which investments in education acquire meaning,
and the subsequent application of a survival strategy, have a number of related
consequences:

- Most students are not intrinsically motivated by the subject matter. The consequence is that students forget much of what they had learned, within several weeks
  after the examination (Van der Werff, 2005).

- There is an increasing lack of motivation in students during the course of their
  study, that is – to a large extent – caused by a poor study and/or career choice
  (Zijlstra and Meijers, 2006).

- As a consequence of this, teachers are forced – often against their will – to view
  pedagogical relations in terms of maintaining an 'orderly, and subject-matter based'
  form of communication. In practice, this means that they (must) invest much effort
  in preserving order (Meijers and Wesselingh, 1999).

- As a consequence of limited intrinsic and continuously decreasing motivation, in
  combination with that fact the student–teacher interaction is reduced to an
  'exchange of knowledge for order' (Willis, 1977), 35 per cent of every cohort, from
  primary vocational education to the university level, leaves school without a diploma
  (even though many do obtain a diploma later).

The fact that many young people 'survive' their educational experience does not imply that they do not learn anything. They, of course, learn something – in addition to survival skills. However, what they learn is – from the viewpoint of the school – largely dependent upon chance: a teacher who does not limit him or herself only to teaching the subject matter but is also honestly interested in the student, a previously existing student interest, the students' background, the support given by the students' parents, and so on.

Self-determination becomes important

For many years, the fact that most young people did not learn for life, but rather for school, was not viewed as being problematical. However, as a consequence of the individualization of society and the transition to a service and knowledge economy, the lack of a future perspective becomes increasingly problematical. An increasing freedom of choice means that individuals are increasingly being forced to make choices. In a society that is becoming less structured, this then leads to more uncertainty (some even speak of a risk society; Beck, 1992). In the individualized society, individuals are expected to be more reflective and self-determining (Giddens, 1991).

Self-determination is the ability to identify one's self (ie., to voluntarily and protractedly associate) with people and organizations, to develop a plan of action on that basis and to implement that plan (Meijers and Wardekker, 2002). When we view self-determination as the ability to associate or relate, it becomes immediately clear that this also involves skills other than only cognitive ones. Of course, an individual must be able and willing to make informed choices, and to delay immediate gratification of needs (affect regulation), in order to develop a long-term perspective. However, an individual must also be able and willing to reflect critically upon the primary relations acquired during primary socialization, as well as the relations that he or she has – consciously or unconsciously – acquired thereafter. He or she must furthermore be able to consider the uncertainty resulting from that reflection, and be able to relate to other concrete people and institutions. The first step requires a mainly cognitive approach: one must be able to find relevant information, process it and draw conclusions. The second step requires an entirely different, more 'literary' approach: it is mainly concerned with determining the central values in one's life, which may become clear by considering one's own personal history and one's 'life story', which is based upon that. The individual also needs to learn to cope with his or her own emotions. This includes both emotions in general, as well as negative emotions, which are inherently associated with distancing one's self from previous relations – and is related to accepting uncertainty. Self-determination is therefore the ability to discover one's own 'life theme' (Van Maanen, 1977) and to relate that to a social role (Law et al., 2002).

Self-determination is not only important due to the individualization of society, but also due to the emergence of three trends. First, the market is becoming increasingly demand-driven, which means that clients not only want 'tailor-made' products, but also that the producer has to take the entire life cycle of a product into consideration. Secondly, there is increasing globalization (the 'global village'), in which time-to-market is of essential importance. The time between product development and the actual production and marketing of the product must become increasingly brief in order to remain competitive. Finally, there is an increasing technological vitality (Korbijn, 2003).

The effect of these trends is that the marketplace is changing constantly and unpredictably, that innovative ability is becoming an increasingly important competitive advantage and that knowledge is of essential importance. In order to survive in this 'booming, buzzing confusion', companies are forced to innovate continuously. They must also apply 'concurrent engineering' in organizing their production, such that employees are simultaneously able to work on multiple product improvements, as well as applying integrated design principles in multi-disciplinary teams. This implies that the organization of labour must become much less hierarchical, and must become more focused on utilizing all of their employees' talents and skills. The organization must become flexible and 'self-learning', which implies not only investment in knowledge management, but also that employees become entrepreneurs: they must be able to manage themselves. This is becoming increasingly important, because traditional career paths are disappearing: the concept of the boundaryless career is gaining ground (Arthur et al., 1999). In addition, in some branches there appears to be an increase in the amount of 'emotional work' (work in which emotions have to be consciously involved; see Hochschild, 1983). For this reason, the educational system has to develop not only the head (theory) and the hands (skills), but also the heart. In order to be able to do that, the educational system will have to develop from being an 'industrial training factory' to becoming a 'career centre', that conceives of itself as a service provider (Geurts, 2007).

Career learning in vocational education

How should educational teaching process and the counselling support for these learning processes be organized such that a school functions as a career centre? This was the guiding question of a study concerning career learning in the primary (vmbo) and secondary (mbo) vocational education in the Netherlands (Meijers et al., 2006).

A powerful, career-learning environment

The research results show that a powerful learning environment for career learning is associated with neither the use of instruments and techniques, nor – somewhat surprisingly – with the presence of a school counsellor. Furthermore, neither the organization of classical consultations concerning study and career choice, the use of career guidance interest tests, nor individual meetings with counsellors or mentors actually contribute to the development of career competences (Kuijpers and Scheerens, 2006) or work identity (a cognitive and affective bond with a specific type of work) (Meijers, 1998). To put it bluntly, the acquisition of career competences and work identity are independent of the use of specific resources or techniques.

What does make a difference is a career dialogue, at school and in the real world. We have defined career dialogue as a conversation that the student conducts with a trusted adult (preferably a teacher, counsellor or mentor), and in which the meaning of a students' experiences for his or her life and career is central. The explicit relationship between relevant experiences of the individual student with the professional/working world and the development of his or her self image and work identity is important. It is essential to stimulate both the internal dialogue (in which personal meaning is central) as well as the external dialogue (in which the social meaning of work is central; see Van de Loo, 2001). Our research results demonstrate that a career dialogue at school and discussions on the work floor, both contribute to three career competences: (1) career reflection (reflection concerning capacities and motivation), (2) career formation (the exploration of career possibilities and the making of conscious choices) and (3) networking. Furthermore, these dialogues contribute to the application of these competences to a concrete choice and learning experience. Both dialogues have even more impact on the creation of career competences and work identity, than do personal characteristics.

A work identity seems to develop mainly by the exploration of career possibilities, and – on that basis – making a well-considered choice with regard to a (study) career: career formation. Thereby, it turns out, again, that the dialogue a student may conduct, in school or in the workplace, is of great importance. Students who conduct such a dialogue have a more strongly developed work identity, than students who do not. There is a clear relationship between the presence of career competences and work identity, and the perceived quality of the choices made. It is also interesting, from the perspective of educational innovation, to note that the quality of the learning environment is also important. Students who receive question-driven training, and/or who are able to conduct a career dialogue, are significantly better satisfied with their choice of study and with the availability of options for school tasks. Satisfaction concerning the choice of traineeships is influenced less by the learning environment inside the school and more by the learning environment at the business involved.

Difficulties with career guidance

On the basis of research (Meijers et al., 2006), one may conclude that there is only a very limited application of well-developed career guidance within primary and secondary vocational education: a 'powerful' career-learning environment was found in only three of the 236 classes investigated. A powerful learning environment is one in which confrontation with real-world problems are central, in which the theories are offered 'just in time' and 'just enough' as an answer to questions arising from this confrontation, and in which the social implications and the value of personal experience in the solution of these problems are discussed with the student.

Meijers et al. (2006) have asked students – as well as their teachers – how career guidance has been concretely implemented. This was done with respect to career reflection (the determination of one's own capacities and motivations) and career formation (the exploration of career possibilities, for example via apprenticeships, and the possibility of giving direction to one's own school career on the basis of work experiences). Almost half of the students (46.9 per cent) were of the opinion that (almost) nothing was done to develop career reflection. Table 3.1 shows that career formation – according to the teachers – is primarily organized by transferring knowledge to the students (34.2 per cent) and by conducting a career dialogue (26.3 per cent). Almost one-third of the students (31.9 per cent) feel that they are left to their own devices with respect to career formation. Only 9.4 per cent of these students say that they have participated in a career dialogue. Furthermore, it is striking that 22.6 per cent of the teachers and 28.8 per cent of the students say that students have no real choices offered to them in the context of their training.

Table 3.1 Guidance in career formation according to teachers and students

Guidance in career formation	According to teachers (in percentage of completed forms)	According to students (in percentage of completed forms)
No choices in learning	22.6	28.8
Students are left on their own	12.0	31.9
Information	34.2	26.6
Advice	5.0	3.3
Career dialogue	26.3	9.4

Finally, this study of career learning in the (v)mbo shows that the present vocational education is still primarily non-dialogical in nature. In recent years, much has been invested in making education more practically oriented, by means of project weeks, excursions, and workplace learning and apprenticeships. However, little has been invested on cultural change (De Bruijn et al., 2005). One of the consequences of this is that career guidance – for all practical purposes – is implemented by only a few, specialized, 'career guidance counsellors' (who are becoming less likely to be a teacher themselves).

The consequence of this development is hardly encouraging for students. The unrelated existence of multiple teaching roles almost always results in multiple behavioural strategies that tend to become increasingly more diverse (primarily because they share little common ground in the primary process). This means the students' task is additionally complex, for they are made responsible for creating synergy (Geurts and Meijers, 2009; te Riele, 2006a). This may be seen clearly by the use of the portfolio. Teachers and career guidance counsellors indicate that they have insufficient time to adequately study student portfolios (Mittendorff et al., 2008). They are therefore forced to assume that students derive their own career lessons from their own portfolio. In a non-dialogical setting, students treat their portfolios instrumentally: they make certain that it satisfies educational requirements. However, they hardly ever look in their own portfolio and they expect absolutely nothing in terms of career planning or guidance (Mittendorff et al., 2008). With respect to the increased demands for reflection, most students react in the same way as they do to the rest of the curriculum: they attempt to make do with as little effort as possible (Holt, 1995). Teachers consequently react to this behaviour by attempting to coerce the desired reflection, by means of instruments such as 'reflection indicators', portfolios and reflection dialogues. Students, as a result, then increasingly view reflection as a school subject.

Educating young people differently: realizing a trialogue

The present interpretation of career learning individualizes the problems confronting vocational education. 'Schools shouldn't want to have a career center, they should be one' as Geurts (2007: 1) aptly remarks. Such a transformation would require the acceptance of a fundamentally different role by all involved:

- for teachers – the change from communicating and teaching study subject matter (the teacher as 'robot'), to the creation of learning environments that allow learners to develop a learning question, which they can subsequently answer themselves ('coach', 'career guidance counsellor', 'learning specialist');

- for school managers – the change from the management of an externally regulated organization oriented towards the production of piecework ('problem solver'), to the design of a learning organization oriented towards the construction of tailor-made products ('problem searcher and definer');

- for students – the change from a reproductive learner ('passive educational consumer'), to one responsible for the development of one's own learning question and – as an extension thereof – of one's own career ('active learning entrepreneur'); and

- for employers – the change from supplier of apprenticeships ('educational Maecenas'), to the co-designer of a powerful and reflective learning environment ('educational entrepreneur').

ROC De Leijgraaf – a school for secondary vocational education with approximately 8,000 students between 16 and 20 years of age – has begun a project that attempts to achieve this role change. The centrepiece of this project is the trialogue between students, teachers and apprenticeship supervisors in the business community. The project is founded on the premise that a powerful learning environment cannot be achieved by the schools alone, for a number of reasons. First, strong 'external leverage' is needed in order to affect change in a non-profit organization (Geijsel and Meijers, 2005). Secondly, career learning is only feasible when students are exposed to relevant and concrete work experiences, and are subsequently able to attach personal meaning to those experiences by means of a dialogue. This dialogue is more productive to the extent that (1) partners are able to trust one another, and (2) the interval between the experience and the reflection upon that experience is shorter (Meijers, 2008). Many students are of the opinion that their teachers have too little knowledge about actual working conditions and the necessary occupational knowledge and skills (Meijers et al., 2006). Ideally, this dialogue should not be conducted in school between student and teacher, but rather in the apprenticeship – the place where most work experience is acquired – between the student and the experienced professional who is acting as supervisor.

Research into the quality of apprenticeships shows that the guidance that students actually receive from their supervisors, is mainly oriented towards occupational socialization (adaptation to the values and norms prevalent in the workplace), and not towards reflection upon the practical work experience acquired there (Meijers, 2003). The primary reason for this is the absence of 'slow motion' time in the workplace.

A powerful career-learning environment seems only possible to realize on the basis of intensive cooperation between schools for vocational education and the regional business community. The existing cooperation between both parties may be characterized as a collaboration based upon 'separate responsibilities': the business community is responsible for making trainee positions available, the school is responsible for the learning process, and both parties stay out of each other's way. In the period 2005–07, the metalworking industry financed a large project that was aimed at intensifying cooperation with secondary vocational education at the regional level. From the evaluation of the project, it may be seen that the development towards more intensive cooperation goes through three phases (van Dam et al., 2007). In the first phase, the cooperation in student guidance takes centre stage: the school and the business involved, together assume responsibility for counselling the individual student, and make specific arrangements for describing who does what, to whom and at which moment in time. Making such arrangements forces the school and business to discuss the (desired) student learning process, and to discuss how those parties – separately, as well as jointly – can support this process. Only when this first phase has been realized can both parties go to the second stage of cooperation in which the creation of learning tasks around real-life problems is central. To make such learning tasks, the school and business have to discuss what 'professional competence' specifically involves, and how that competence is concretely implemented in that particular business. When the school and business are able to make concrete arrangements for the guidance of specific students, and together develop learning tasks, then they are also capable of further developing this cooperation to the level of 'mutual innovation'. In this last phase, a discussion may arise concerning how those professional skills will develop in the coming years in a specific branch. This implies that a discussion must be conducted concerning how the relevant market will develop, and which technological advances may be anticipated. Based on this discussion, a process of interactive knowledge transfer may develop between (mainly) smaller and medium-sized businesses, and vocational education.

A practical strategy is to make occupational dilemmas a subject of discussion. Occupational dilemmas are the daily-occurring, practical, occupational role-conflicts that are caused by the divergence of the scientific-technical, the cultural-political and the economic discourses that determine occupational practices. An occupational dilemma reflects the tensions between:

1. The economic and scientific-technical discourse: an occupational practice can be improved, but this does not happen because it is not economically profitable. Consider, for example, the perpetually burning light bulb that Philips has invented – according to rumour – but does not market because this would mean the financial ruin of Philips.
2. The economic and cultural-political discourse: an occupational practice is con-

stricted with respect to its meaning for economic reasons, while simultaneously the need exists for richer forms of meaning giving. Consider the caregiver or nurse for the elderly, whose primary task is doing the housework. However, at the same time, it is expected of these caregivers that they take the time for a good conversation with their clients/patients, in which the perspective of that client/patient is central.

3. The cultural-political and the scientific-technical discourse: in occupational practice, technical innovations are possible, yet are not acceptable (or have not yet been accepted) from a cultural-political viewpoint. Consider the debate around modern gene-technology.

By discussing these relevant occupational dilemmas with their supervisor (and others in the company), students are able to find an initial answer to the three central questions concerning their career: 'What kind of person am I?', 'What type of work would be suited for me?' and, finally, 'Can I be the type of person that I would like to be, in this company, and in this segment of the labor market?'

Discussion questions

1. Think about your own school career. How often have you had the experience that you were really learning for life?
2. Teachers are generally much more positive about the extent of dialogue with students, than students are themselves. How can you explain this asymmetry?
3. Self-direction requires the development of the mind, the hand and the heart. How much room is there in modern education for the development of the 'heart'?
4. Is it really necessary that education and the business community cooperate intensively?

Further reading

Collin, A. and Young, R.A. (eds) (2000) *The Future of Career.* Cambridge: Cambridge University Press.

Website

Bill Law's Career Learning Café: www.hihohiho.com

Note

1. In the Netherlands, after primary education (4–12 years), 60 per cent of the pupils move on to primary vocational education (vmbo) and 40 per cent go to

general secondary education (havo and vwo). The vmbo education lasts four years, the havo five, and the vwo six years. In the Netherlands, there is statutory compulsory education until 18 years of age. Thereafter, 90 per cent of the vmbo graduates move on to the secondary vocational education (mbo) and 10 per cent go on to the havo. More than 80 per cent of havo graduates move on to the tertiary vocational education (hbo) and 20 per cent to the vwo. More than 75 per cent of vwo graduates go to the university; 25 per cent of them go to the hbo (CBS, 2007).

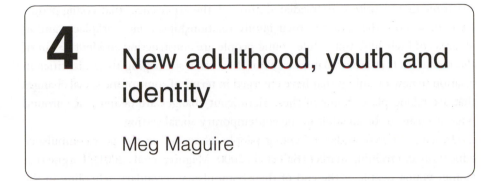

4 New adulthood, youth and identity

Meg Maguire

This chapter argues that some young people who are less successful at 'doing school' will construct alternative identities that sustain their sense of self. These identities are also mediated by changes that are taking place around adulthood. The chapter:

- describes the dominant identities on offer at school;
- suggests that some young people construct alternative identities that sustain their self-worth;
- argues that dominant discourses surrounding older versions of adulthood might be redundant to the identities that young people are constructing for themselves; and
- considers the related policy context in the UK.

Identity matters

The making up of identities is a reflexive process. Identities are products of multiple, and often conflicting, discourses and practices. They are subject to aspects of biography-identity such as family and interests, culture and style. While individuals construct their identities out of the structural and material resources at their disposal such as the inter-sectionalities of class, race and gender, their identities are inflected by the constructions being made of themselves by others, and by/against the identities that are on offer in the social world. Youdell (2003: 19) has pointed out that identities can be 'constrained within mobile discursive chains that can act to trap particular identities in ways that are counter to or at odds with the intent or desire of the individual subject'. She claims that some young people can become 'trapped' in particular versions of identities 'which seem almost impossible to escape' and which may not be of their own choosing. White and Wyn (2008:

12) argue that identities are 'mediated' through the experiences that young people have 'in schools, the nature of their family relationships, their workplaces and in all areas of their life'. But, while young people are constructing an identity out of the resources that are available to them, they are also shaping their identities in relation to new meanings that have emerged in terms of some of the social changes that are taking place. Some of these significant changes are taking place around what it means to be an adult in the contemporary social setting.

Drawing on two studies of young people 'choosing' in the post-compulsory education and training market (Ball et al., 2000; Maguire, et al., 2001), I argue that (some) young people at the end of their compulsory secondary schooling in the UK are less able and perhaps unwilling to produce dominant identities of the 'good' student. In contrast, changing imperatives in their social and cultural settings, notably in the construction of prolonged adolescence and new adulthoods, mean that some young people are constructing and being constructed through identities that sit uncomfortably with dominant versions of the 'good' student. Those young people who are less successful at 'doing school' and who are less able to 'accomplish' themselves as successful learners may produce alternative identities that sustain their sense of self and personal esteem. In particular, dominant discourses – identities on offer perhaps – surrounding older versions of adulthood, and adult responsibilities and roles, might be unattractive and less available and, thus, redundant to the identities that some young people are constructing for themselves. Some of these older versions of adulthood may provoke anxiety, distress and discomfort in some young people.

School – the best days of your life?

Many students enjoy school because of the opportunity to meet their friends and peers; teaching and learning may be somewhat less important. However, even if students do not always hold pro-school attitudes towards the academic side of school life, if they are moderately successful, they will have more reason to stay in the system. 'Less successful' young people are more likely to be offered 'damaged' learner identities in school, and repeatedly, and early on in their learning careers, may get messages about their academic failure and reduced worth (Reay and Wiliam, 1999). In a school system that celebrates attainment and success, some students may well become impelled to make up a different identity, one that carries more promise of esteem and value. In the extract below, Debra provides an account of what schooling is like for her, and perhaps for many other students:

Well, sitting in lessons every day and listening to teachers telling you what to do, that isn't really enjoyable is it? [...] And finding the work hard isn't enjoyable either is it?

And teachers that don't help you, don't make it enjoyable do it? So I don't get much out of this school, do I? (Debra)

In a recent study in the UK, Archer et al. (2007) tracked 89 young people who were 'at risk' of dropping out of education and training. Many of these young people constructed identities that were based on fashion, style and consumption 'as a means for personal valorization and mobility – a chance for individuals to "be" or feel "better"' (Archer et al., 2007: 224). Some young people in our studies (Ball et al., 2000) constructed similar identities. For example, Michael had moved out of mainstream school where he had been bullied. 'I just had an interest in clothes. I knitted a cardigan, and jeans, loads of clothes I made myself.' As we wrote, 'he is making himself up, so to speak, through the clothes he makes and buys, through his hair style and through his body sculpting at the gym' (Ball et al., 2000: 32). Education (in school) had not offered Michael an identity that was either desirable or valued. His interests and vocational aspirations were not part of the mainstream school curriculum (but see Chapter 5 by Stokes and Wyn in this volume, which offers an alternative case study of positive identity work in school).

Those young people, who find schooling less rewarding, less enjoyable and a place that speaks to them and others of their personal and academic shortcomings, become compelled to produce an alternative identity that sustains their feelings of self-worth. But, while I recognize the various ways in which they can make up positive identities that may reduce negative emotions and perceptions, their identity constructions will inevitably and inescapably be mediated by structural and material factors. Young people, who are perhaps in danger of being excluded by their schooling, and from their schooling will not be able to make up any identity that they 'chose'; inter-sectionalities of class, race and gender will circumscribe the identities that they construct. Simultaneously, these young people will be also be constructing their identities out of, and perhaps against, the discourses of adulthood that are on offer.

Youth and new adulthoods

The so-called 'transition' from youth to adulthood has changed in some significant ways (Ball et al., 2000; Furlong and Cartmel, 1997; te Riele, 2006a). Flexibility, deregulation, privatization and constant change and reform, characterize the current labour market condition (see Stokes and Wyn, Chapter 5 in this volume). In the northern hemisphere many manufacturing jobs and skilled apprenticeships have been shed. With deindustrialization has come a growth in the financial and services sector. Educational qualifications are increasingly seen as the passport into the world of work – a shaky, risky world where low-pay jobs in care, support and services predominate, and where downsizing and outsourcing threaten the viability of occupational stability in many settings.

Young people do not now leave school and move into the same occupations as their parents. For one thing, there are far fewer jobs available for school leavers. In the UK, policies are in place (and are currently being ratcheted up) to compel young people to stay in education and training beyond the compulsory leaving age – there are few social welfare benefits available to unemployed 16-year-olds. For another, older forms of transitions that were frequently gendered, such as trades, skills and manufacturing, are less evident today. Indeed, with the rise of service sector occupations, young women are far more readily employed than males (Ball et al., 2000). Jobs are not for life; young people have to depend on parents and carers for longer periods of time.

There have been significant changes in the sociocultural setting. Many young people in the UK live in single-parent households or live in families made more complex by changes in partnerships, divorce and step-relationships. As the family structure has shifted, it is less likely that families will have the support of localized traditional networks of extended kinship, although there may be a need for extended dependency on the family. Whereas in the recent past, 'adulthood and independence have been constructed as successful entry to the labour market and this has been normalized in class terms' (Maguire et al., 2001: 201) the situation is far more complex today. Older transitions between youth (as measured by participation in education) and adulthood (full-time participation in work) have dissolved. In many ways, there is a 'new adulthood' where young people will more characteristically experience fluid, uneven transitions between youth and adulthood.

A recent study of young adults in Bristol, a prosperous city in south-west England, argued that these new forms of adulthoods characterize what they call the 'adaptable generation' (Bradley and Devadason, 2008). In their sample of 78 interviewees who were aged between 20 and 34, 'this generation of young adults (were) more dependent on either their families or the state than was the case with previous generations' (ibid.: 130). Bradley and Devadason (2008) found that there was a high degree of 'interdependence' taking place for an extended period rather than separation and independence. As they say: 'The flexibilisation of the labour market has indeed created a precarious economic environment, which hampers people's prospects of achieving the conventional markers of full adult status: financial and housing independence and stable employment' (Bradley and Devadason, 2008: 130–1).

For some young people, the vista of choice, fluidity, expansion and lack of early closure may be a positive and enriching period. In our studies (Ball et al., 2000), some of the young people certainly were located in the immediate and were living for the moment. For example, Anne just wanted to have a great social life and her immediate ambitions were centred on this: 'I would like to have my own place, my own personal space and do what I want when I want, invite all my mates around whenever I want.' Anne's views exemplified a perspective that was 'tak(ing) refuge from a daunting future in a focus on an extended present' (O'Connor, 2006: 120). For others in our studies, the world of adulthood and responsibilities did not always seem an attractive proposition. Fiona had not liked school and had dropped out in the last year of her compulsory education. What she said reflected a great deal of anxiety about who she was and what she thought she was supposed to try to be (a grown-up) as well as her desire not to have to take responsibility:

> I still feel as if I am a little girl […] I feel very young and not sure of myself […] I feel I should be making all these decisions I am not ready for […] other people are making these decisions like jobs and college and I just don't want to have to. (Fiona)

Lucy's comments demonstrate the ways in which the pull of the immediate coexists with the inevitability of the future – a future that might not be attractive to some young people.

> Long ago people had to grow up like really early and go to work and pay money into the house and whatever. But now you might as well have fun this age because you are going to get serious as you get older […]. When you settle down and have children and a job and all that, it becomes more serious and grown up and I'm not ready to be a grown up yet. I just want to enjoy myself.

What these extracts suggest is that young people may not be the rational, calculating individuals that governments 'imagine' in youth transition policies. All the young people in our studies generally subscribed to the value of qualifications and education and training – but were not always committed to participation right away. Amma talked of wanting to find work rather than staying on in education: 'I didn't really feel that I wanted any more education. I know that you should want to stay in school or go to college. Everyone says that you should get qualifications, but I didn't really feel like that. I felt that I was ready to work.'

In their study, Bradley and Devadason (2008: 131) found that young adults were 'living with insecurity; anticipating instability over their lifetimes, their general framework of expectations is very different from that of their parents'. Similarly, in our studies with young people in London, we found a more flexible and 'relaxed' attitude towards the future and employment:

> My brother always tells me to get an apprenticeship to learn something. I don't know. I would rather just stay myself, do what I want to do. I appreciate that they help but

they tie you down [teachers]. I just want to do what I want to do and change my mind if I want. I don't want people telling me what to do all the time. I've had enough of that at school. (Rees)

Current policy moves

Previously in this chapter I suggested that high-stakes testing and outcomes-driven values in schooling were likely to position and identify students as 'good learners' or alternatively as students with damaged learner identities. In practice, empirical work demonstrates that the construction of learner identities in the school setting is far more complex than this binary would suggest; Youdell (2006) talks of the positions between 'acceptable and unacceptable' learner identities. Nevertheless, in schools it is ability that is highly valued – and in schools this just means academic aptitude. Other talents and strengths are not factored in.

In the UK setting, each summer national newspapers publish tables showing which schools have 'done well' in the tests. News items regularly show groups of happy excited young people hugging their friends and all celebrating their success in the end of school examinations. All this triumphalism places almost impossible pressures and feelings of shame and reduced worth on those who cannot claim these successes. Even though some students 'avoid' the possibility of 'failure' through leaving school before final examinations (as some did in our studies), by making friends with older people outside school to boost their self-esteem and self-worth (as some did) or through constructing a version of adulthood in respect of sexuality/drugs, messages of success (and failure) are in circulation in the media, the students' friendship groups and other networks. If schools (and the wider population) are seen as valuing product over process, then inevitably some students (possibly those more likely to do less well) may take up ego-defensive strategies such as withdrawing, staying at home and rejecting any further education and training, and constructing alternative and more affirming identities. Yet it is this cohort who are (and always have been) on the receiving end of policies that concentrate on reintroducing them to education and training, after in some cases, nearly 11 years of being constructed as having a 'problem learner identity'.

In the UK there are long-standing concerns about disaffected youth and the 'long tail' of young people who are not in education or training once their compulsory schooling has ended at 16. These concerns are compounded by high levels of youth unemployment due to the lack of available work for young people without formal qualifications. These concerns are also driven by claims that many of the 25 per cent of young people in this cohort lack the skills that are needed in the contemporary labour market. There is also concern about this cohort of young people who are not in post-compulsory education, employment or training (and currently referred to as NEETs) (DfES, 2000) in terms of social 'problems'. The recent Green Paper, *Raising Expectations: Staying in Education and Training Post-16* (DCSF, 2008b), points out that individuals will benefit by staying on in education and training in terms of enhanced earnings over their lifetime. In addition, 'those who participate are less likely to experience teenage pregnancy, be involved in crime or behave anti-socially' (DCSF, 2008b: 12). One result is that the UK government has announced that it is to raise the school-leaving age to 17 by 2013 and then to age 18 shortly afterwards. (It is expected that legislation will be introduced in spring 2009 in order to facilitate this change). There will be a push to ensure that all young people participate in education and training on a voluntary basis but if, after different sorts of support, they do not participate:

> We propose that the young person would be issued with an Attendance Order specifying the provision they must attend, where and when. This would be a civil, not a criminal process. Only on breach of this Attendance Order would there be a question of sanctions, through either a civil or a criminal process. (DCSF, 2008b: para. 27)

As Norris (2007: 472) argues, 'a key issue will be how the motivations of young people can be harnessed to make a success of education and training beyond 16'.

On face value, raising the school-leaving age and compelling all young people to stay in education and training for a longer period seems to be a sensible strategy to try to ensure that more young people gain credentials and additional skills. Indeed, many western societies are advocating similar policies. However, drawing on a range of international studies that demonstrate the diversity and complexities of youth transitions, Ross and Gray (2005: 124) claim that age-based models of educational provision are 'increasingly out of touch with the realities of young lives'. They suggest that policy-makers need to recognize the ways in which young people make up complex, individualized narratives and identities in the contemporary social world. These identities may not all include an educational or training dimension that moves neatly onto a predetermined age so that young people can all be chronologically 'propelled through the education system in quest of a credential and as a result obtain employment and contribute usefully to the economy' (Ross and Gray, 2005: 124).

Policies of raising the compulsory leaving age are predicated on a discourse of rational choice theory – that all young people will make a 'sensible' choice in their best economic interests – they will want to continue in education and training. There is also an assumption that young people's choosing is a decontextualized activity; that factors of social and material disadvantage can be easily managed away. However, choosing at this point of transition may be more complex. For example, in our studies, some of the young people were managing and navigating through complex and sometimes chaotic situations. Some were caring for their parents; others were bringing up children, or coping with emotional and social complexities such as substance abuse and homelessness. For those who were trying to manage an emotional biography of complexity, where schooling was at best a distraction and at worst a place where they felt abandoned, excluded and shamed by their lack of success, choosing to do more of the same would almost be counter-intuitive. Where the prospects of older versions of adulthood (work and independence) were less available, and perhaps somewhat 'scary' too, making the 'right choice' and staying in the system might just not have been an attractive or emotionally viable proposition for some young people. Staying in the system may well be in the long-term best interests of those young people who currently reject this offer, but the way this choice is positioned in the *Raising Expectations* document may be missing the point: in accenting an economistic identity, they may be displacing other more desirable 'learning identities for living' (see Stokes and Wyn, Chapter 5 in this volume).

Doing education differently?

For those who have been alienated by their previous schooling in an academic and competitive system, the opportunities offered by a further two years [...] may have to have as little resemblance as possible to that previous schooling. (Allen and Ainley, 2007: 131)

If young people are going to be expected to stay in the formal educational and training system for two additional years, as determined by their chronological age and not necessarily their choice, one issue relates to what types of young people are being imagined and positioned as the subjects of this policy intervention? In terms of those who see staying on in post-compulsory education and training as a 'normal' part of what 'people like us' do in terms of achieving a traditional version of 'adulthood', there will be little change, although perhaps if new courses are offered there may be some erosion of the academic–vocational divide. Those young people who Allen and Ainley (2007: 131) recognize as being 'disaffected by their schooling' and who urgently need to be brought in 'from the margins of society', need adequate financial support and an entitlement to a curriculum through which they can 'pursue their cultural and intellectual interests whether or not these are related to their employment'. For example, the Australian case study in Chapter 5 in this volume details ways in which the performance arts curriculum can support young people in 'living well'. However, in terms of the current UK policy recommendations in this area, delineating an age-specified and non-voluntary requirement to participate sidelines what is already known about the perceptions, experiences and lived identities of these young people. Some young people may be keen to return to study in their twenties or even later. Others may not yet be ready to commit to any 'career decisions' or choices other than living in the present.

Doing education differently would mean taking seriously the real changes that are taking place in society and that are reframing new constructions and experiences of adulthood. Jones (2002) suggests that if we are serious about educational policies that are aimed at young people, then we perhaps need to start from a different perspective. Her argument is that policies that position young people as the 'problem', deftly sweep aside the 'very real problems that society and social problems present to young people' (Jones, 2002: 39). Damaged learner identities produced by school experiences will not be easily overcome by merely providing more of the same. Debra pinpointed this dilemma: 'So I don't get much out of this school, do I?' If the provision is just more of the same, then it is likely that Debra, and others like her, will still get very little out of what they are offered.

If young people are to construct more positive learner identities, then they are going have to be able to experience and achieve success (a broader version than is currently on offer in a credential, outcomes-driven educational setting). In a time where many of the policies that address young people are constructed on 'outdated and false assumptions of "youth", too few take real account of the family context of young people's lives' (Jones, 2002: 39). In a world where transitions between youth and adulthood may be fragile and fracturing, and where older versions of adulthood are redundant, for policies to be effective they need to start from an appreciation of how things really are for many of the young people who are the subjects of all these endeavours. Schools, as currently constituted, may not be the best places to support this identity work.

Discussion questions

1. What types of learner identities are available in schools? How significant are these identities for different social groups?

2. In what ways has adulthood changed and what influences do these changes have on identity construction?

3. What types of non-coercive policies could extend opportunities to young people like Debra and Fiona?

Further reading

Bradley, H. and Devadason, R. (2008) 'Fractured transitions: Young adults' pathways into contemporary labour markets', *Sociology*, 42(1): 119–36.

White, R. and Wyn, J. (2008) *Youth and Society: Exploring the Social Dynamics of Youth Experience*. Melbourne: Oxford University Press.

5 Learning identities for living

Helen Stokes and Johanna Wyn

This chapter argues that identity work has become increasingly significant to young people's transitions through education and work. The chapter:

- discusses the impact of late modernity on the kinds of identities that young people must forge;
- argues that there is a gap between narrow, economistic educational policies that focus almost exclusively on matching skills to national economic needs and the realities of young people's needs for life-wide and lifelong learning; and
- presents a case study of how education can provide the resources for young people to engage in productive identity work through the performing arts.

This chapter explores the question of what young people need to know and learn in the twenty-first century. We argue that mass secondary education continues to reflect assumptions that informed its establishment half a century ago, and has not kept pace with change. By contrast, in later modernity young people have had no choice but to learn how to live with new realities such as labour market unpredictability and the fragmentation of traditional pathways though education and work. We argue that in late modernity, identity has become a task rather than a given, and identity work has become an essential part of the equipment that young people need to negotiate their way through an unpredictable world.

Educational researchers highlight the importance to young people of 'becoming somebody' and of understanding 'who am I and who is "us"?' (McLeod and Yates, 2006: 12), both within and outside formal education (Smyth and McInerney, 2007). In response, identity and subjectivity have become a central question in contemporary educational research as educationalists explore the ways in which subjectivities are shaped through education and the ways in which young people do the work of shaping identities (Henderson et. al., 2007; Kelly, 2006; Stokes and Wyn, 2007; Youdell, 2006).

Educational policies have also responded to changes in labour markets and economies. However, these changes have (paradoxically) tended to reinforce older understandings of the role of formal education as primarily a means for producing the skills and capacities to serve 'knowledge' economies (OECD, 2007). There is an emerging gap between policy directions that position the role of formal education as a tool for the economy and the ways in which young people are using education – as part of a repertoire to live and thrive in a context of uncertainty.

This chapter discusses the significance of identity work for young people and illustrates the role that education may play in supporting young people to engage actively, reflectively and critically with subjectivities. The first section discusses the importance of identity in late modernity and makes a case for schools to provide young people with more effective resources for identity work. The second section provides a case study illustrating how an arts-based programme, working with young people some of whom feel marginalized from school, enables young people to feel connected with learning, with each other and with their school community.

Young people and identity in late modernity

Young people in western countries face increasingly complex trajectories, options and pathways through education, work and life (Furlong and Cartmel, 1997; White and Wyn, 2008). Changes in many aspects of society since the 1970s (which mark the beginning of the period called late modernity), have meant that young people must chart their own routes and negotiate new sets of risks in the form of 'personal' choices (Bauman, 2001; Furlong and Cartmel, 1997). Changes in the relationship between employers and employees (including contract employment and the creation of a 'flexible' labour market) mean that young people bear the risks of changing skill requirements and of uncertain markets. Young people feel the need to hold their options open and to become flexible workers in order to manage precarious labour markets, even in times of high employment.

Learning has also become more complex. Formal education has become more flexible, so that young people have choices (sometimes a bewildering array) about the timing of their formal education, and it is now common for young people to take a 'gap' year or two before or during their higher education courses. The articulation of degrees across different sectors (for example, in Australia between secondary school, technical and further education and university) also opens up choices for young people. Young people are also both workers and students, establishing a pattern of balancing study and work in secondary school that they will continue throughout life (Stokes and Wyn, 2007). Learning is 'lifelong' and 'life-wide' as young people learn in workplaces, through their leisure pursuits and in informal educational settings as well as through formal education.

Of the many elements that contribute to the importance of identity work two key elements are the process of individualization and the rapidity of change. Individualization is a term used to describe how, in late modernity, as the structures that create inequality and uncertainty have become obscured, individuals have come to feel responsible for the associated risks. An example is the way in which Generation X faced economic recession when they emerged onto the labour market, but became a vanguard generation in terms of their acceptance of the ideal of being a flexible, mobile worker (Stokes and Wyn, 2007). Identity work is crucial to this new approach to work and to a life based around uncertainty. It involves the capacity to be self-reflective and to be aware not only of the occupational skills required for entry into particular occupations, but of the attitudes, ways of relating to others and ways of presenting the self.

Rapid change has also made identity work crucial today because in a context of uncertainty, in which security is not guaranteed through external processes (such as having a credential or gaining a job), personal capacities and personal development have become increasingly significant as a way of ensuring survival. This involves the capacity to reinvent one's self to respond to changing workplace requirements, and to be capable of performing constantly to demonstrate one's worth and to establish fulfilment and meaning through having a balance between work and life. As Beck and Beck-Gernsheim point out, as collective identities that were characteristic of industrial societies have begun to lose their relevance 'needing to *become* what one *is* is the hallmark of modern living' (2002: xv, original emphasis).

Identity-making takes centre stage as young people strive to manage these complexities. There are a number of ways in which young people learn to negotiate the risks of late modernity. For example, Giddens's concept of 'autobiographical thinking' highlights the capacity to narrate and create one's self-history as a central aspect of identity-making, that is a fundamental characteristic of contemporary identities (Giddens, 1991: 54). Bourdieu's concept of habitus has provided a framework for understanding how particular dispositions and embodied ways of being in young people are differentiated by class, gender and race, and how these elements of identity may be supported or contradicted as young people interact with school and the particular 'school ethos' (Bourdieu, 1976). Foucault's concepts of 'governmentality and technologies of the self' (1988) underpin the idea of the 'enterprenurial Self' – an ideal encompassing the sets of attitudes and capacities of the young person who is 'self-managing' in the face of uncertainty, is future oriented and who accepts personal responsibility for making the right choices (Kelly, 2006).

New subjectivities have become dominant in late modernity, as some ways of being have become more effective than others. Success is related to the capacity to engage reflexively and continuously in the processes of constructing themselves as choice-makers and to demonstrate that one takes individual responsibility, is resourceful and a reflexive, enterprising subject (Rose, 1999), regardless of age. These subjectivities are an essential resource base for the successful negotiation of education and labour markets in new economies, as well as other aspects of life. Although there is not space to consider this issue within the scope of this chapter, it is important to note that some groups of young people (especially young women from high socio-economic backgrounds) have been especially responsive to the need to perform particular identities, and some groups (especially young men from low socio-economic backgrounds) have found this more difficult (McLeod and Yates, 2006; Stokes et al., 2004; White and Wyn, 2008). New patterns of inequality of outcomes based on class, gender and geographic location are formed as some groups are more able to draw on cultural and economic resources than others to secure success.

Young people understand that gaining educational credentials will not guarantee them a job and that they must actively construct education and employment biographies that make them attractive in precarious and changing labour markets. Most importantly, they understand that while employment can provide a basis for economic security, it is important to have a balance in life – to have space and time for friendship, relationships, leisure and enjoying life in the present. Hence, the individualization of responsibility for creating effective pathways through life has heightened the relevance of subjectivities and the task of actively constructing one's biography. Identity work has become a significant new dimension of learning in late modernity.

Learning and identity work in the performing arts

The performing arts play a key role in the construction of youth identities. Participation provides young people with the space to begin to negotiate their place in the wider world. The knowledge and skills gained in programmes such as creativity, networking, group skills improvisation, learning to learn and flexibility are highly appropriate for the changing demands of the labour market and young people's individual biographies (Miles, 2003).

This section of the chapter presents a case study based on the experiences of a group of young people living in the inner western suburbs of Melbourne (Australia) attending a performing arts programme that was provided as an extra-curricular activity at their school after school hours. The school is in a geographical area of Melbourne with one of the highest rates of early school leaving in the state. The performing arts programme caters to young people from a diverse range of cultural backgrounds. It links with the school to provide an after-school programme for young people, some of whom are disengaged with school and are deemed to be at risk of leaving school. While many of the young people volunteer to attend, some are encouraged by teachers at the school to attend. The programme has a team of artists who work with the young people after school hours to create a performance drawing on the life experiences of the young people. Two teachers from the school attend rehearsals and assist with school organization.

The case study, which was developed as part of an evaluation of this performing arts programme (Stokes, 2003) illustrates the role of drama in enabling young people to engage with identity work. The programme explicitly sought to develop reflexive skills and access identity resources and stories based on their own lives that would assist them to live well.

Involvement in the drama process involves not just gaining skills in drama performance but being able to make links between the content the young people discuss and create, their world and the larger world of which they are part. Young people's narratives and their ability to develop those narratives is an important aspect of how they negotiate their own biographical projects (Giddens, 1991). It was important that they could link their own stories with a larger world view. This is because when knowledge has a link to a young person's life it becomes more meaningful and accessible. Storying one's life is a learned practice, a reflective practice … and schools can be instrumental in the development of such practices (Stokes et al., 2004: 29).

Through the drama processes and the development of a performance that expresses what the young people want to say, discussion of issues is generated and alternative ways of dealing with issues that impact on the lives of the young people are developed. These include the discussion of violence, drug use, gangs, peer pressure, relationships and family relationships. As artists who were working with students in the performing arts programme commented:

> The young people are looking for a means of understanding their society and their role within it.

> [It] should be stuff that is relevant to them and that they have actually experienced so it should start out from where they feel a real link too. They're starting from where they're at.

This view is spelled out in the aims of the drama programme that are to empower young people to express their thoughts and feelings through art and, by doing so, deepen their understanding of themselves and society (Stokes, 2003).

As the artists and students collaborated to write a play using characters developed by the young people, they constantly worked through a process that encouraged the students to 'work out differences of opinion and beliefs and accept divergent perspectives of those around them' (Waldorf, 2002: 22). This attention to the perspectives of others, the capacity to negotiate difference and to express one's own views offers students a powerful tool for identity work. In their lives they are required to respond to multiplicity and contradictoriness at any one time and identity construction is a process of negotiation among different parts and times of the self and among different settings (Melucci, 1996). The structure of the script they developed contributed to this complex process of identity development through attention to making choices. For young people in the postmodern world, having to navigate choices and the choices that are made play an increasing importance in developing identities and subjectivities (Brooks, 2006) where 'the modern individual is not merely free to choose but obliged to be free and to enact their lives in terms of choice' (Rose, 1999: 87).

The process of identity work is illustrated through the discussion between two of the young people, who explain that using group work to develop characters, everyone gets opportunities to put forward ideas and choose different points of view. For these young people it is an opportunity that does not always happen in the classroom. As one of the young people explained:

> You do stuff you are happy with doing. You can use your own ideas, you get your ideas heard and they all get put into the story whereas in everyday school it's just not as good because you can't always get your opinion heard if there are 25 people yelling and screaming and you are trying to get your voice over the top of them.
>
> Everyone can get their ideas across. When the big group has now been divided into small groups we sit in a circle and everyone gets their ideas across and sees which one is good. The artists help us out with what we want to do. They ask us what we want to do and then we tell them and give them ideas and we all do it. Then we all come back in and show it to everyone. We do separate themes. We choose and everyone is comfortable. It's the students' ideas that get scripted out.

The other student commented:

> They go around and see what people think. Just chuck around ideas and they listen to every single person in what they have to say. It's great. We split into groups and each one of them can listen to each person's point of view.

The process of character development is explained in more detail by one of the artists:

> They were told that also we'd be pulling stories from their experiences and they seemed quite happy about that so I just think it's about just creating different types of structures that will enable stories to come out through role play, through improvisation, through discussion, through kind of character-based exploration that can lead to story.

Another artist explains the complex role they play in facilitating the young people making choices and exploring those choices:

> As artists we have constantly to consider the choices that the young people will make and whether they are genuinely empowering. If they decide to push the narrative towards dead-ends in terms of moral/political outcome then the play has not challenged preconceptions nor has it explored the full complexity of human behaviour, it is simplistic wish fulfilment.

Initially the script reads like a teenage drama show on television but at the same time is dealing with issues that some of the young people are facing and that concern many of the young people.

The artist went on to explain:

> It was kind of like a social drama, that type of genre. They were engaged with the story and I think they did quite well because from an emotional investment point of view they had to invest in order for the story to be credible and considering the age group they really sustained that I think.

She commented further on the depth of the material that the young people were exploring:

> We're dealing with fairly potent material, it's not like you know you are just dealing with something like shopping. It requires a level of commitment in sincerity in terms of what they're doing and the fact that they were asked to play adult roles like a doctor or a mother or father.

The arts programme has also promoted an understanding of different cultures (Matarasso, 1997). For example, a student in the programme used the workshop process to explore her culture, which she felt was different from most of the other students. The parts of her culture that were both important to her and causing internal conflict for her were included in the play through the character that she developed. She said that this made the character 'more real and important to her'. There were a number of negative influences that she felt were coming from her family and culture that placed constraints on her. She felt that daughters in her family were treated like prisoners and were being spied on by male members of the family. Being involved in the drama programme allowed her to share her concerns with others and to express the ways in which her family situation and her wider cultural context were both a source of support and a source of limitation.

The artists explained drama techniques that were used to allow both exploration of the issues the young woman is experiencing as well as protection from judgement about the character she is creating.

Empty chair – *protection into role*

To help establish the character of a young woman who feels imprisoned at home by both family and cultural expectations, an empty chair is set in the space and the artist-in-role as the parent can talk to the chair as if the girl was sitting there and anyone in the group can answer as the girl from where they are sitting. They provide her voice, but don't physically represent her. A different person may provide the girl's voice with each response.

The artists have found that the use of the 'empty chair' *protection into role* techniques (Bolton, 1986) can be a powerful way of exploring sensitive issues, while giving the group the safety they may need.

As soon as a character is established and named he or she becomes the property of the group that created him or her and is quite distinct from the actor who may portray him or her in a given moment. The artists commented that understanding and highlighting this process is an essential protection that stops young people 'acting' as themselves and therefore being exposed to comment and judgement. The facilitator must constantly make decisions about how close to a particular young person, a character should be allowed to go.

It was important for the artists to make sure the young woman did not alienate herself from her own culture and family in the process of creating her character that had meaning for her. As this was to be a public performance that her family might attend, the writers worked with her to protect her by rewriting her character to still portray her difficulties but to bring in some of the positive aspects of her culture. For example, her brother was rewritten to be still keeping an eye on her activities, but because he loves her and wants to protect her, rather than as a 'spy' for her father.

One of the artists said:

> When we write up stuff I think we are aware of who is, what they were interested in or what do they do well and what did they really connect with and then building from that so that they're able to go beyond their levels of experience.

While one teacher described the storyline as being very conventional, at another level she found that 'it works for the kids in terms of working out challenges'. Through the role plays and improvisations the young people are able to explore the complexity and multi dimensional nature of relationships that they are experiencing.

Playing multiple roles and working through complex relationships through involvement in this type of self-generated drama process allows the young people to engage in important identity work that is required of them in a changing society in which 'the abundance of possibilities and the messages thrust upon us all serve to weaken the points of reference on which our identity is based' (Melucci, 1998: 184). Education has an important role to play in providing what Falk and Kilpatrick (2000) describe as 'identity resources' – self-confidence, trust, shared values and vision and commitment to community. Developing a broader notion of curriculum that includes arts-based learning as a core element also promotes a greater depth of understanding. As one of the young people said:

> We break up into groups and we develop stories and then we actually perform them, whereas (at school) we might just think up something and leave it at that. It's getting into groups and dwelling on it and spending an enormous time on it and get really good. It is altogether different from what we usually do.

Conclusion

While there has always been some degree of responsibility on individuals to negotiate their own path through education, work and life, the scale of the shift towards dependence on individual resources in late modernity has made this a defining feature of young people's transitions. Responsibility for learning is shifting from the educator to the educated.

In as much as educational policies have recognized the need for education to respond to social change, this has tended to rest on traditional assumptions about the preparation of young people to serve the economy. This has created a disjuncture between educational policies that continue to frame education within an industrial model (instrumental and vocationalist) and the requirements that young people themselves have for the capacity to be good navigators through new economies, to live well, and to engage with complexity and diversity. This means that personal and social development has achieved a new significance as an element of the skills and capacities that schools aim to support young people to learn.

The case study of how identity work is supported through the performing arts provides one example as to how school can provide young people with the increasingly sophisticated personal repertoires that they require to manage their lives. It offers a challenge to educational policy-makers to recognize the needs of young people for learning experiences that equip them to engage with immediate issues, rehearses the exercise of choice and decision-making, and enables them to link school learning with their personal lives.

Discussion questions

1. Discuss the impact of individualization on young people's lives. Is it the same for all young people?
2. What opportunities do young people have for identity work outside school?
3. What activities at school provide opportunities for identity work?
4. What could schools do to provide/recognize opportunities for identity work?

Further reading

Brooks, R. (2006) 'Learning and work in the lives of young adults', *International Journal of Lifelong Education*, 25(3): 271–89.

McLeod, J. and Yates, L. (2006) *Making Modern Lives*. Albany, NY: State University of New York Press.

Stokes, H. and Wyn, J. (2007) 'Young people's identities and making careers: young people's perspectives on work and learning', *International Journal of Lifelong Education*, 26(5): 495–511.

Vaughan, K., Roberts, J. and Gardiner, B. (2006) *Young People Producing Careers and Identities: The First Report from the Pathways and Prospects Project*. Wellington: New Zealand Council for Educational Research.

6 Doing identity differently in practice

Kitty te Riele (Case study 6.1)
Frans Meijers (Case study 6.2)

Chapters 3, 4 and 5 have provided scholarly views on changes in youth identity and ways in which schooling can respond and contribute constructively to these identities. These have focused on vocational, school and life identities, in the context of choice biographies, as outlined in Chapter 1. This chapter incorporates two practical case studies that demonstrate how education may be done differently in response to the issues raised about young people's identity.

By coincidence both case studies are from Dutch settings, however their ideas are relevant internationally. The first case study is based on an alternative senior high school. The second case study is provided by Frans Meijers, illustrating arguments he outlined in Chapter 3.

Case study 6.1 EigenWijs: schooling for living
Kitty te Riele

EigenWijs is a small senior high school established in the Netherlands in 1983 (all translations from Dutch by Kitty te Riele, with apologies for any errors). Although young people arrive at EigenWijs for many different reasons, they tend to bring with them negative identities gained in (and often provided by) their previous school(s). These include being disruptive, a truant, a bully, or a victim of bullying. Such labelling is an extension of the authority of teachers to 'diagnose', identify and categorize students. The first obvious difference between EigenWijs and other schools is thus in the terms used. Instead of 'teachers' and 'students' EigenWijs refers to 'co-workers' (*medewerkers*) and 'youth'. As the school explains: 'The various participants in EigenWijs are on an equal footing. In this vision, the youth literally become workers, and the others co-workers' (EigenWijs, 2008a: para. 4).

Moreover, the school's own name has a double meaning. While *eigenwijs* is an adjective literally meaning opinionated in a headstrong kind of way, by using the double capital, EigenWijs, the school also hints at another meaning: Own

Continued

Continued

Wisdom. Taking seriously the fact that despite earlier unpleasant experiences the young people are still willing to learn, the school thus focuses on the strengths and interests that each individual young person brings. This is the first step towards both recognizing and contributing to more constructive identities.

To make sure that names and terms are not just tokenistic but symbols of deeper differences in how the school works with the young people, EigenWijs follows up on this first step with a range of other initiatives. The key principles underpinning EigenWijs are respect and shared responsibility.

When a young person starts at EigenWijs, they are offered several days for orientation. The purpose is very much reciprocal, demonstrating two-way respect, for both school and young person to gain an understanding of each other. This is followed by a trial period of several months during which the young person is supported by a mentor.

The way schooling itself is organized within EigenWijs also reduces the opportunity for negative identities to be formed. Tests and homework are negotiated between co-workers and young people. Punitive disciplinary measures such as 'penalty tasks' and detention are unknown. On a larger scale, while in Dutch secondary schools it is fairly common for students to be told to repeat a class (a highly visible stigma) EigenWijs does not have traditional year-group classes but small groups, so that 'repeating' is not an option.

Groups are largely organized around whether the young people are expected to take final examinations at the end of that year or not – but young people can take some subjects in the examination and others in the non-examination group, completing their full diploma over several years. Other groups are based on themes, unrelated to examinations, which may include anything from photography to philosophy. Finally, various groups take on a project chosen by young people to develop new interests or to build on old ones. Projects are intended to be active, for example making a video, cooking or sport.

EigenWijs explains its focus as follows:

> We consider it important that young people (re-)gain grip on their own lives, and can make independent choices, take responsibility for these and learn to justify their actions. At EigenWijs much attention is given to young people's personal development. Many of these things are present in activities which we collate under the heading 'living'. (EigenWijs, 2008b: para.1)

Projects fall under this heading, because they are in part aimed at mutual cooperation. There is also a weekly conference during which young people can raise issues or make suggestions for the running of the school. Finally, young people and co-workers together clean the school building daily and weekly – one

Continued

Continued

of the few compulsory activities at EigenWijs. The responsibility extended to young people led one of them to explain: 'It is not really a school but more an organization of which I am also a part' (Drop and Volman, 2006: 20).

While the school helps young people to achieve a senior high school diploma, this is not the only aim. Recognizing that a young person's identity goes well beyond school, EigenWijs encourages the development of young people into independent, creative and social individuals who can survive in society, not separately from societal norms and values but in a way that is their own.

The final words go to a young person and her parents, in letters to her old school which form the introduction to a book about EigenWijs (Drop and Volman, 2006: ii):

> Remember me? Ilonka from 4va. I am doing much better now but it still feels rotten. I was so confused, and you were so powerless. 'All bastards' and an 'unable to be supported child'. It just didn't work together. (Ilonka)

> We hardly dare to say it but it's going well now – we have found each other again. It was unacceptable that all these years we could not help our child. We are her parents after all. And what could you do as the school? Why were the early signs not picked up, why was there so little time? Why was there so much suspicion? Dear EigenWijs gave her her own place, gave her a feeling that she is just fine, that she has the right to be who she is. (Ilonka's parents)

Case study 6.2 X-stream learning: follow your dream

Frans Meijers

The Friesland College, a school for secondary vocational education with approx-imately 15,000 students (16–20 years) and 1,150 employees, decided in the mid-1990s that all educational processes would be implemented as 'experience-driven learning' (EDL). The reason for this far-reaching innovation was increasing lack of student motivation. This was demonstrably caused, in part, by teaching being primarily theory driven. Experience-driven learning was initially imple-mented as 'problem-driven learning': teachers formulated problems that were then solved by the students, step by step. Theory was presented in the context of the presented problem. Evaluations of problem-driven education demon-strated that students were more motivated by this form of teaching than by traditional forms. However, dropout percentages were hardly affected. Problem-driven education was still viewed by students as being excessively formal.

Continued

Continued

In 2001, a new unit was organized in which all learning processes would be driven by actual professional practices. This unit, the so-called FC–XL (Friesland College – Extreme Learning, the name created by the students themselves), begins the learning process with the execution of concrete and realistic tasks. Students may choose from a large number of available tasks in order to allow them to orient themselves with respect to various vocational fields, and, in this manner, to develop their career. With every concrete task performance, the student may reflect upon the tasks executed (under the watchful eye of a specially trained coach) with the goal of clearly enunciating the specific knowledge and skills needed in order to perform that task. Thereafter, the needed knowledge and skills will be acquired under the supervision of specialists (teachers as well as experienced professionals from local businesses).

Within the EDL, actual professional practice plays a vital role. The students' learning motivation is limited when they begin XL. Many students arrive in the XL project because they prefer to be practically employed, and have a strong resistance to everything resembling formal schooling. XL counselling attempts to connect to the learning style of these students, for most of whom concrete experiences are central. Coaches must ensure that students reflect upon their experiences. Friesland College works closely with regional businesses and institutions, which is essential for the central assumption of the FC–XL: learning is done best in the real world.

The school year involves four periods of 10 weeks in the FC–XL model. Students work on assignments for nine weeks; the tenth week is in 'slow motion', intended for students to draw their own conclusions. Students are given feedback, primarily by the coaches but also by the content specialists. During the school year, various learning and counselling activities are utilized: 50 per cent practical training supervised by coaches and teachers who are content specialists, 20 per cent theoretical background supervised by content specialists, 20 per cent counselling aimed at improving self-reflection and supervised by coaches, and 10 per cent activities not related to vocational training (such as music or drama).

When students are of the opinion that they have sufficiently developed one or more competencies, they may request a 'panel discussion'. Participants include not only the teacher-content specialist (who presides as chairperson of the panel), but also a coach and an expert (experienced craftsperson/professional) from a local company. The judgement of external experts is especially important, for they determine whether they consider the student to be a potential trainee or even a colleague.

Continued

Continued

The examination commission ratifies this judgement and determines whether there is sufficient evidence that the national examination requirements are met.

One's own career is central

FC–XL assumes that students determine their own career. The coach guides the student in forming a coherent learning experience. The educational programme is concluded with a recognized diploma. The programme begins with an interview, in order to determine which competencies students have already acquired and what their future vocational ambitions are. The coach and the student then go to work, determining the steps needed to be taken in order to achieve those ambitions. These ambitions constantly guide the selection of practical and theoretical learning activities. FC–XL assumes that working and learning in the real world stimulates students' intrinsic motivation, whereby they can steer their own learning process, under supervision. Students also receive support in order to develop their own personal qualities.

Coaches play an important role. A coach supervises and supports the students' learning process from beginning to end. In this manner, they are able to build up a relationship with students, which enables the coach to reflect upon the learning career of each student, as well as to encourage students to reflect upon themselves. Each coach counsels about 15–20 students. An important difference with other programmes in the Friesland College is that, in the XL programme, the roles of the coach and the teacher (who is a content specialist) are separated. As it turns out, few teachers are able to fulfil both roles. A good content specialist is not necessarily a good coach. In addition, when a teacher attempts to fulfil both roles, the danger exists that the coaching role may be underemphasized, when more attention is needed for the content. In the XL programme, the content specialist assists by the development of occupation-specific expertise, while the coach assists the career development of the student within the vocational context. The coach gives no instruction for the development of occupation-specific expertise, but does help to organize this process, to formulate learning goals and to reflect upon real-world experiences.

Extensive evaluations – conducted by the Friesland College itself – demonstrate time and again that FC–XL students are better motivated and learn better than the average Friesland College student. A national survey of the development of career competencies also showed that the XL offered the most powerful career learning environment of all schools studied. In 2006 XL won the National Innovation Prize for Vocational Education, an award established by the Dutch National Department of Education.

7 Embedding the ethic of care in school policies and practices

Kumari Beck and Wanda Cassidy

This chapter posits that schools based on the ethic of care offer a radically fresh approach to engaging youth in learning and in the school experience. The chapter:

- provides a brief introduction to the ethic of care, showing how care focuses on relationships, empathy, other-directedness, dialogue and respectful solutions;
- provides some examples of how educators have enacted care in their schools; and
- argues for a pedagogy of care, which will build an inclusive environment where all students can succeed and grow.

Opinions on schooling and teaching proliferate, with ideological divides on how schools should be run 'differently' from the way they operate. Changes proposed range from bringing back the 'small school', to arts-based or other specialization schools, schools that provide learner-centred environments, to schools that stress examinations and traditional forms of instruction. Common among these opinions is the assertion that schools are 'getting it wrong'. While we agree that school does not work for a variety of students, we believe that 'doing school differently' must be based on the needs of students and serving those needs relationally. Many students appear to be alienated from learning, from one another and from the adults they are supposed to be learning from. Too many students feel unwelcome and unwanted at school, and find that they are not receiving the help they need to succeed and thrive educationally and socially (Cassidy and Bates, 2005). School seems irrelevant and disconnected from students' lives, resulting in many students dropping out or being 'pushed out' (Fine, 1991; Wotherspoon and Schissel, 2001). There is some recognition of the problems but in general 'solutions' are sought through pre-packaged programmes, applied as add-on strategies in ad hoc fashion, but rarely are the roots of the issues addressed.

There is wide agreement that schools and communities should be caring places, and caring, we contend, should provide the basis for teaching practice. We have selected the ethic of care as the framework or foundation for developing pedagogy, because of its suitability to our overall vision of building a community-based learning environment that serves all learners. 'The current structures of schooling work against care, and at the same time, the need for care may be greater than ever' (Noddings, 1992: 20). Schools that align with ethic-of-care approaches look at creating the right culture, or the right soil, so that students may thrive, rather than looking to behaviouristic models or rules and consequent approaches for managing the school and containing student behaviour. Teachers and school administrators are encouraged to model and practise those values and behaviours that they wish to see emulated in students. Thus, ethic-of-care approaches aim to be holistic and pervasive, becoming embedded in all school policies and practices.

No one, least of all in the teaching profession, would say they are uncaring, and everyone would likely say they care about their students and that they want them to be successful. This popular notion of care lulls us into a complacency that having *intent* to care will make schools into caring places. Furthermore, care is often perceived simply as 'being nice'. Ethical caring in all its complexity is still not widely understood by teachers and administrators and, therefore, is not widely practised in school settings. To understand caring as pedagogy, one must have a sound understanding of the principles of ethical caring.

In this chapter, we first introduce, briefly, some of the basic theory on the ethic of care as conceptualized by Nel Noddings (1984, 1992, 2002). These elements of care will be illustrated through examples from teachers and administrators who are integrating the ethic of care into their practice, developing a pedagogy of care. These examples are part of a research study Enacting the Ethic of Care, undertaken in Western Canada. Much has been theorized about the ethic of care, but little research has been done on its enactment in teaching/learning environments. In our study, 14 teachers and administrators from a variety of educational settings (elementary, secondary, alternate, post-secondary; inner-city, suburban, rural; multicultural; diverse socio-economic levels) participated in a community of inquiry, over four years, that sought both to understand and explore the practices and conditions that would support them in initiating and sustaining the ethic of care in their day-to-day school lives. The main findings of this study relate to how teachers and school administrators perceive and cultivate caring within themselves, with colleagues and among students, and how policy and practice have been influenced. While it is not possible within the constraints of this chapter to write extensively about the findings themselves, nor the wide-ranging implications for practice and the theory, we do offer a few examples of how these educators practised an ethic of care. We conclude by discussing the implications of this approach on developing a pedagogy based on the ethic of care.

What is ethical caring?

Caring for others is a natural impulse in humans. Natural caring is directly observable and experienced in the family, between mother and baby, and parents (and extended family) caring for their young. The motivation to care, according to Noddings, 'arises on its own' (1995: 187), and thus natural caring is accessible to all. The question that scholars such as Noddings address is how this natural caring can be extended to become ethical caring (1984) so that care is not limited to private life, but can be widely practised in public life (2002). As Noddings argues:

> The custom since Plato, has been to describe an ideal or best state and then to discuss the role of homes and families as supporters of the state. What might we learn if, instead, we start with a description of best homes and then move outward to the larger society? (2002: 1)

Indeed, the question that relates to educators is how can we understand what it means to bring ethical caring into the classroom as a fundamental aspect of schooling?

Care is a relational ethic, with an emphasis on 'living together, on creating, maintaining positive relations' (Noddings, 1992: 21). Acknowledging the work of Gilligan (1982), Noddings articulates care as a 'needs and response-based ethic' (1992: 21) which involves an encounter or connection between the one caring, or carer, and the cared-for, or receiver of care. The carer perceives that there is need for care and is moved to respond with a caring act. This impulse to care becomes ethical caring in the relationship between the one who gives, and the one who receives care. The cared-for participates by 'receiving' the act of care through response, or reciprocity. Ethical caring in these terms offers opportunities for people to connect with one another 'in relationships characterized by mutuality' (Noddings, 1992: 18).

Caring, then, is 'not a specific set of behaviours' (Noddings, 1992: 18) or attributes, although there may be virtues that support care. It is constituted in the *relationship* between the carer and the cared-for, and this participation of both carer and cared-for in the act of caring marks ethical caring as an ethic of relationship and mutuality. The inclusion and active participation of the cared-for also ensures that caring cannot be codified, nor can the carer refer to a set of 'rules' or a template, as each act of caring demands a unique response generated from the specific needs of the cared-for. Thus, the ethic of care calls for *seeing* ethical possibilities in everyday

context

experiences; caring results from our sense of connection with each other, that is, of community. From the position of being cared-for, at one time, and from practising care as a carer, it is possible to develop this capacity. It is a memory of being cared for, or caring, or an ideal of ourselves as carers that enables the carer to act.

As moral education, Noddings (1984, 1992) articulates ethical caring in terms of four elements: modelling, dialogue, practice and confirmation. Modelling and practice are both concerned with 'growing' the capacities to care, and highlight the importance of providing caring opportunities so that carers and cared-for alike can develop their capacities to care. The labels of carer and cared-for are not fixed identities, which allow the cared-for to become habituated to care first through experience and then through subsequent practice. Thus, the modelling of care has the effect of letting students know they matter and giving them an experience of what it means to matter, and provides the cared-for with good memories and experiences of caring encounters. It also has the effect of spreading 'good practice' outside the classroom by habituating the cared-for to engage in ethical caring themselves. Practice and modelling promote and nurture the enactment of care and they cannot occur without dialogue.

Noddings (1984) uses the Freirian concept of dialogue as a vital aspect of a caring practice. Dialogue, as Freire (2000) articulates, reduces the power imbalances and 'contradictions' inherent in the teacher–student relationship. Open-ended dialogue where the intention is to 'receive' the other, and 'attend' to the other through empathic listening, enables both sides to move to new co-understandings that have the potential to break through the most intractable of positions and situations. Dialogue may also involve the unspoken word: touch, smiles, affectionate sound, silence or glances, 'a feeling with, and attending to' (Greene, 1991: 544). Dialogue from a caring perspective is never coercive, and always invitational, 'a common search for understanding, empathy or appreciation' (Noddings, 1992: 23).

The fourth element, confirmation, is not separate, and often arises from dialogue and is conceptualized by Noddings, in Buber's terms, as 'the act of affirming and encouraging the best in others' (Noddings, 1992: 24). Confirmation requires 'seeing and receiving the other'; for example, the teacher clearly sees what the student did, receives the feelings with which it was done and chooses the best to attribute to that student, while at the same time nurturing the student towards the ethical ideal (Noddings, 1984: 196).

Enacting care: rewards and challenges

In our research on the ethic of care, we sought to understand how the theory on the ethic of care, described briefly above, was perceived by educators and enacted in classrooms and schools, and if we could identify elements of a pedagogy based on the ethic of care. Developing relationships with students, and finding the time to build community in their classrooms were top priorities among the teachers and administrators who were invited to participate in our study. Care, for these educators was primarily about 'getting to know each [student] as much as possible' as expressed by Kaylin. 'It means being genuinely interested in their lives,' emphasized Denise, a vice principal in the same school. As she continued, 'Care cannot just be words; it must be followed by tangible action'. The 'action' she spoke of is the response that follows from perceiving the needs of each student, and in her experience, the more one knows students, the better the ability to perceive and respond actively to needs.

As Noddings describes, there is 'no recipe' for caring, and '[c]aring teachers [need to] listen and respond differentially to their students (1992: 19). While this is one of the most important features of an ethically caring approach, it also leads to one of the most significant challenges to maintaining care in a classroom with large numbers of learners of diverse backgrounds, with curricular and other demands, and the unique needs of the students themselves.

Relationship and community building were addressed at a number of levels and with a variety of strategies among our participants. Problems relating to exclusion and marginalization begin from very early ages, as observed by our educators, resulting in divisions and attitudes being more firmly established by the time students enter high school, vocational and alternative school, and post-secondary institutions. In their view, the absence of a caring approach in early education contributed enormously to problematic learning and social situations in later teenage years. Having a broad representation of educators in our study provided the bigger picture of how care contributed to the well-being of students, or the lack of care to problems related to marginalization and exclusion. The elementary teachers illustrated how those problems could be addressed early in the educational life of students, while the educators from alternate schools provided lessons to be learned from successful approaches in their environments.

Ken, a school counsellor and teacher in an alternative school programme, expressed it well:

> If care was a more central characteristic of the school, perhaps some of the social issues that affect at-risk students could be addressed more effectively. If educators really care about at-risk students dropping out of school then more flexibility in scheduling and perhaps less instructional classes and more self-paced ones could help individual students living in less fortunate personal and social situations.

Ken suggested that care should become more 'mainstream' in all schools, rather than an alternative practice in an alternative setting alone. Identifying belonging and recognition as primary needs among all students, and in particular among marginalized and 'at-risk' youth, he continued, 'If more at-risk students could feel a sense of belonging and recognition within the school community this would hopefully in turn encourage them to participate more fully within it'. Enacting care within a classroom and school, in Ken's experience, meant creating opportunities and strategies to foster that sense of belonging, and to recognize all students in the classroom. These in turn connect back to the notion of knowing, respecting and valuing the student, leading to a mutual relationship between educator and student, discussed earlier.

Some of the more moving descriptions of the transformative effect of care were from educators who worked in alternate settings, serving students who were marginalized in multiple ways. Helen (teacher) and Peter (principal) in a school for at-risk youth related how the youth they served were able to learn only because of the efforts made to first establish trust and connection. In their experience, the ethic of care offered hope to these students in difficult situations. 'Often, this is the only thing they have to hold on to – that someone cares for them and what happens to them' (Peter).

Ken offered hope to his students by confirming them through unconditional positive regard (a concept based on Carl Rogers). Ken saw the presenting behaviour of these youth as a result of a lack of care in their lives, and unmet needs. One of the ways in which he met that challenge was to introduce a pet-care programme in which the youth took responsibility in caring for a pet, thus gaining experience of physically caring for another being. The work of restoring healthy relationships in their lives is an enormous task, but one that must be addressed. 'It's modelling … you are modelling how people can interact with one another [in a healthy way]. It's not like forcing your agenda, you are just "being"' (Ken). Helen also reinforced the 'being with' students as an essential element of a pedagogy of care:

> [M]ostly it is just about being with them. And that's such a vague term, but be with them, be interested in their lives and I do that every day … play cards with them, take time just to hang out with them … tell them a little about my life … that's how I develop a relationship with them. (Helen).

This 'honouring them through treating them well' (Helen) often resulted in a dramatic shift in how the students themselves responded to the programme, and to school. With these successes however, our participants recognized the enormous effort, energy and time that were required for a pedagogy of care, and they returned often to the topic of self-care and sustaining practices of care.

The monthly meetings in our research group served as a venue in which the participants talked through these and other dilemmas that presented themselves in the practice of care. Denise and Kaylin convened a teachers' dialogue group in their school to examine what practices and conditions supported teachers to sustain dialogue that centred on care and inclusion. They studied and discussed the work of Nel Noddings and then worked through their own challenges to care. An important outcome of this initiative was the realization that care of the self through dialogue and support generated from the group was critical in sustaining practices of care. Also, care of others entailed the knowing of self, increased awareness of self and others, and the ability to increase the capacity to perceive and understand the needs of others.

Care, as these teachers discovered, is complex, and requires support, time, and a holistic and integrated approach in its enactment. Among the teachers in our study (including ourselves), we discovered that dialogue deepens understanding of ethical caring, and deepens practice as dilemmas and problem situations are discussed and worked through, and the learnings incorporated into everyday classroom teaching. It was evident that the capacity to care is connected to reflexivity. In other words, attending to the other, is to see one's own role in the caring relationship. Here we particularly refer to the power relations embedded in the teacher–student relationship, and how one's power influenced and affected the mutuality of the relationship. As Peter explained:

> You let *them* define the relationship … I don't have a relationship model that I'm going to have with all the kids coming in, and what I have is 'This is who I am, how do you want us to be together' … and I try to be approachable so that any [student] feels like they can approach me on whatever level, and some kids, you know, it's a very minimal relationship, and that's all they want, that's all they need. But … they know that I'm there, and they can come to me and that may be all that they want.

Perception or 'seeing' is another critical aspect of ethical care. Teachers must be skilled in perceiving needs rather than, for example, projecting their own ideas of student needs. And so, care relations are grounded in being able to see ourselves, as well as developing capacities to see inwardly and outwardly. Other-orientation requires a high degree of self-reflexivity and self-knowledge, and these are key qualities in the development of a pedagogy grounded in care.

Administrative support and leadership in setting a tone and approaches aligned to an ethic of care were key factors in furthering a pedagogy of care school-wide. For three administrators Janice, Sarah and Elaine, this meant balancing and constantly navigating among the needs of students, parents, teachers and other support persons, while keeping clear the objective of supporting students to be successful in school. Learning in the classroom, according to Sarah, is not an isolated cognitive activity. It is dependent on everything else that is going on in that student's life. A pedagogy of care for all the principals meant leaving their doors open at all times so that students could wander in whenever they wanted to ask questions, share something exciting or simply check in if they felt moved to. 'The kids come to you with their problems and they'll talk to you, and you can go into a classroom and the kids will quiet down, and they'll follow your direction – because you have that connection' (Janice).

Sarah and Elaine worked in schools with high immigrant populations, and both commented extensively on the correlation between students who are successful learners and a caring environment with strong relationships at all levels of the school. As Elaine comments:

> You can have the most wonderful curriculum, the most wonderful methodologies in the world, and if a [student] doesn't like his teacher or doesn't feel safe with his teacher he's not going to learn to the best of his ability. So kids have to know that people in the school care about them. And care enough about them to see beyond just what they present, you know. To know enough that a raised eyebrow, or something like that might signal 'I'm feeling anxious' or 'I'm stressed. I'm needing some attention'.

All the administrators in our study emphasized this role of creating connection with the students in their school. For Elaine, 'Care means considering all the angles, and sometimes bending the rules a bit. You know, looking after people rather than looking after policy sometimes'.

An ethic of care can be enacted in a variety of ways – an orientation to ordering school, designing the curriculum around a model of care, caring for ideas, care as critical learner engagement and caring for the world around us. We have not addressed here issues regarding caring and the curriculum, but wish to point out that there is much for exploration. In fact, it offers a clear alternative to what we consider an undue emphasis among teachers and student-teachers (in particular) on lesson plans and methodologies.

> How do we move the system to recognize that teaching and school is more than reading and writing? ... And get teachers to move away from the curriculum? ... Educators are a product of the culture of conformity and obedience ... of math tests and homework. This is not school, and this is not learning. (Denise)

And for at-risk youth, Ken articulated clearly how an ethic of care could bring about change and school success: 'If an ethic of care were more central to the education curriculum, at-risk students could be able to learn things that they actually care about. Being allowed to study things that interest them would likely make them feel more cared for.'

Conclusion: towards a pedagogy of care

The data emerging from our study strongly confirmed the value and benefits of establishing a community that provides its participants with ample opportunities, resources and support to examine, reflect on and transform their practice towards a caring orientation. We found that the enactment of care leads to capacity-building of educators' ability to sustain practices of care and that we may actually learn, despite the challenges to our narrow boundaries of self, to perceive and emotionally respond from the place of deep ethical caring for the other, and in particular the significantly different other. Care theory focuses attention on the concept of self as a relational one and the ethic of care enables us to combine the cultivation of ethical self with practices that are congruent with important goals of education, in the development of 'good' human beings. As one of the participants summarized, 'caring practices are about the well-being of others' (Wendy) and the research meetings led to a strengthening of our capacity to both understand and navigate through the messy world of practice, 'the courage to walk a different road' (Wendy).

Our participants found the journey towards enacting the ethic of care into their schools and classrooms immensely rich and fulfilling, a journey worth continuing. Each talked about their own lives being enriched and deepened, about a strengthening resolve to seeing ethically caring possibilities in their interactions with students and in the decisions they made each day about what to teach, how to teach and how to foster interpersonal relationships among students and colleagues. Several talked about feeling empowered in their classrooms and about being excited to see their day unfold. They were able to see their role in the school with greater acuity.

Rawls (1971), in his book *A Theory of Justice*, claims that education must be judged against the standard of how well each 'educated' person has improved the situation of those who have lost out. Greene (1991) argues that an education based on caring brings with it a vision of healing and an unleashing of people's ethical power to act for the betterment of all. As discussed by our research participants, this path is not easy, but 'it is too important to ignore' (Kaylin). What we have seen in our study is that enacting the ethic of care in schools not only makes school a better place for students and teachers in the 'now', but has the potential to impact the wider community as students and teachers engage with more distant others in ethically caring ways.

> **Discussion questions**
>
> 1. Using examples from your own schooling and teaching, describe what constitutes ethical caring.
> 2. How do modelling, practice, dialogue and confirmation facilitate an ethic of care?
> 3. What are some of the challenges faced by teachers in practising a pedagogy of care, and how do these limit the enactment of care?
> 4. In what ways does this chapter encourage you to think more deeply about enacting the ethic of care into your school or educational institution?

Further reading

Noddings, N. (1992) *The Challenge to Care in Schools: An Alternative Approach to Education*. New York: Teachers College Press.

Palmer, P. (1998) *The Courage to Teach: Exploring the Inner Landscape of a Teacher's Life*. San Francisco, CA: Jossey-Bass.

Recommended viewing

'Dare to Care: Transforming schools through the ethics of care' (2009), DVD directed by M. Hawley and D. Van Poelgeest and available through the National Film Board of Canada (www.nfb.ca).

8 Pedagogy of hope

Kitty te Riele

This chapter proposes an innovative pedagogy, based on philosophy of hope. The chapter:

- explains the concept of hope, and argues that hope should be complex, attainable and sound;
- sets out the pedagogy of hope, based on four resources: a positive culture of learning, focusing on possibility, establishing a community of hope, and critical reflection; and
- provides practical examples drawn from research.

In Greek mythology, the idea of hope goes back to the story of Pandora, who was given a jar by the Olympian gods. The jar was full of evils which were released into the world when she opened it. Pandora quickly shut the jar and only one thing remained inside – hope. Does this mean hope is imprisoned? Or is the jar keeping hope safe, preserving it as an antidote to evils?

Teachers can recognize both possibilities. Faced with a lack of resources, 'troublesome' students and/or increasing workloads it can seem that there is no hope – it is locked away. On the other hand, faced with such difficulties, teachers can equally feel grateful that hope exists – a positive resource to help them. Goleman (1998) agrees with the second interpretation when he argues that in stressful jobs hope is a crucial asset. This chapter focuses on pedagogy of hope in relation to teachers, but the suggestions can also form a generative source of action for others working with young people.

The idea of hope

Interest in using the idea of hope in education ranges from 'hope theory' in psychology (Snyder, 2002) via pragmatist (Shade, 2006) and critical (Biesta, 2006;

Giroux, 2003; Halpin, 2003) philosophy to social-transformative pedagogy (Freire, 1994; McInerney, 2007). The pedagogy proposed here is largely based on a synthesis of pragmatist and critical contributions, together with the philosophy of human hope outlined by Godfrey (1987).

Teaching is sometimes seen as a 'discipline of hope' (Kohl, 1998). This sounds uplifting, even inspirational. But too often such use of hope tends to lack analysis of what hope means or how it may benefit education. The predicament here is that 'hoping is often conflated with wishing and thought to be some kind of magical palliative, simply invoking the language of hope does not take us very far in addressing real problems' (Shade, 2006: 193). While the intentions of well-wishers may be good, such idealism is likely to lead to false hope. In education, this is of particular concern when students have already experienced disadvantage and disappointments. On the other hand, foreclosure of hope (Giroux, 2003) is dangerous too. When teachers hold deficit assumptions about disadvantaged students the mechanism of self-fulfilling prophecy (Rosenthal and Jacobson, 1968) can operate. Therefore, we should neither give *in* to false hope nor give *up* on good hope.

For hope to be beneficial in education it needs to meet three criteria: it must be complex, it must be attainable and it must be sound. Too often hope is used simplistically, as Grace (1994) argues, to celebrate examples of certain students and teachers succeeding against the odds. The flip side of celebrating such individual successes is that failures also are attributed to individuals: students who have not tried hard enough, teachers who have not implemented solutions properly. Since the influences on schooling are much more complex than that, hope also needs to be more complex. This means taking seriously not only the agency of individuals and groups, but also the social structures that shape schools and society.

This leads to the next point: hope must be attainable. While hope inevitably involves obstacles, hope also assumes that these can be overcome – otherwise we would give up. In education, especially for disadvantaged students, a focus on hope carries the risk that it will 'only exacerbate our feelings of disconnection' (Shade, 2006: 214) if hope seems unattainable. Attainable hope is located between wishing and planning. Godfrey (1987: 14) points to the definition by Aquinas of hope as 'what is agreeable, future, arduous and possible of attainment'. Hope is both more agreeable and more attainable than mere wishful thinking. Hope is also arduous – if it is easy to achieve we do not need hope, we can simply plan to make it happen. This means that 'there is a tension between desire and expectation, and it is this tension that helps make hope transformative' (Sanders, 2007: 5).

Finally, hope must be sound. Even with complex and attainable hopes 'we should not take for granted the goodness of any hoped-for end' (Shade, 2006: 194). While it is an important first step to refuse to accept a difficult, wrong or bad situation as inevitable, the next step needs to consider whether an alternative hoped-for situation is necessarily better (Biesta, 2006). This means pedagogy of hope requires an ethical evaluation. Godfrey (1987: 2) explains sound hope as: 'hope that is positively linked to human well-being'. This is a major distinction from psychological hope theory which is explicitly neutral about the value of hoped-for goals (Snyder, 2002). Sound hope is essentially social because it seeks 'the flourishing existence of the other' (Godfrey, 1987: 29) – of relevance to teachers since this parallels a key aim of education (Collinson et al., 2000: 24).

Pedagogy of hope

In education 'there is no guarantee that the teacher's hopes coincide with the student's' – and reconciling these hopes involves 'hard work, patience, and courage' (Post, 2006: 274). The pedagogy of hope needs to involve both teachers and students, clarifying what is hoped for and the ownership of those hopes. This section outlines four suggestions for specific resources that contribute to the pedagogy of hope:

- a positive culture of learning;

- focusing on possibility;

- establishing a community of hope; and

- critical reflection.

These are illustrated by examples from published research and from two Australian research projects: A and B (see Acknowledgements for details). These examples are intended to illustrate possible ways of using the pedagogy of hope, without denying that teachers' agency is constrained by the institutions, systems and society in which they work. It supports a fundamental disposition to work towards a better future based on 'a realistic appraisal of current conditions [as] a starting and not a terminal point' (Shade, 2006: 212). In other words, not giving up because of difficult conditions (of poverty, discrimination, disadvantage) but rather grounding hopes in an analysis of these conditions to enable an intelligent 'engagement with the possibilities of change' (Halpin, 2003: 20).

A positive culture of learning

Schools that demonstrate a positive culture of learning tend to highlight strengths, not only in terms of academic performance but a broad range of accomplishments (Collinson et al., 2000), and on effort, improvement and community spirit. This culture involves a shift: 'moving from a problem-focused deficit model in which only a few kids are considered intelligent enough to become well-educated to an empowerment model in which all children are validated for their unique strengths and abilities' (Benard, 2004: 25).

The school that took part in project A has found it vital to celebrate their successes, since they are often perceived negatively as 'a school for those who can't handle school' (as a student put it). For students and staff, such celebrations boost self-confidence and provide energy and inspiration. It also helps make the community aware of results achieved despite the challenges they face. For example, prizes won by the Bantam chickens bred as part of the vocational education programme and participation in a formal debating evening with other schools demonstrated the strengths of both the school and students.

In contrast, working in an Aboriginal community school in Australia, Sarra (2003: 4) found that teachers emphasized the 'cultural and social complexities' that impeded student performance. Such views can (unwittingly) sabotage a plan to foster achievement and build hope. Sarra (2003: 4) decided that 'If change were to occur, the school had to change its beliefs about what our children could achieve, and our children had to change their beliefs about what they could achieve'.

Creative imagination helps teachers to perceive the possibilities in young people, not just the 'deficits'. A remedial reading teacher applied this imagination:

> One of my students, I believe that I've really, really succeeded with him because when he came I asked him to identify why he wanted to read and he wanted to do a scuba diving course and he realized that he couldn't read the questions on the paper. So I actually taught him to read the scuba diving manual, that was his reading. And we sat there every week and went through the scuba diving manual and he, look, he was reading words like compression and depressurization – getting it all right, it was great. (Project A)

A culture of building on strengths not only helps students (especially those who all too often have been seen as failures) to clarify and realize their hopes, but also provides satisfaction and new energy for teachers.

Focusing on possibility

While holding on to unattainable hopes is demoralizing, the reverse is just as appalling and much more common: to give up and to have others give up on you. Halpin (2003: 21) argues that fatalistic expectations about the ability of some children (and some schools) to do well 'are the scourge of an education programme premised on hopefulness'. Pedagogy of hope focuses on alternative possibilities rather than statistical probability: 'If we follow probability there is no hope, just a calculated anticipation authorised by the world as it is. But to "think" is to create possibility against probability' (Stengers, in Zourzani, 2002: 245).

For students from disadvantaged backgrounds Shade points to the importance of countering the 'discrimination of lowered expectations' (2006: 208). Teachers often lower their expectations with good intentions: to avoid frustrating or embarrassing a student they think is unable to perform a task, and thus preserve their self-esteem. Yet, such actions by the teacher simply reinforce any perceived deficits (Gale and Densmore, 2000) – students who are never asked to complete challenging tasks never get the chance to learn to do them. When low expectations are based on background (gender, class, indigeneity) whole groups are being disadvantaged.

A teacher in a regional Australian high school (project B) exemplified positive, high expectations for students statistically perceived as unlikely to do well in school (low socio-economic status with many of indigenous background) especially in her subject: Japanese. The challenges to setting high standards and making the subject meaningful were substantial. Nevertheless, students were engaged, enjoyed the lessons, and learnt. One lesson focused on the Japanese words for various body parts, including the 'head, shoulder, knees and toes' song in Japanese.[1] The class went though several rounds of practising the song pointing to the relevant body parts, with decreasing teacher support. Eventually, students began to volunteer to perform the song alone. The others cheered them on even when they forgot one or two words, and those who managed the whole song received thunderous applause.

This teacher set challenges for students and enabled them to succeed, but she acted largely in isolation from her colleagues. The dominant deficit perception, blaming students for their poor performance, placed structural constraints on the influence of her more hopeful pedagogy. Focusing on possibility is more powerful when it is part of a school-wide ethos, which requires a school leader enforcing a strong counter-discourse, as exemplified by this high school principal in project B: 'I don't think anyone in this school would be game enough to say to me you can't do it with these kids because they know it's head ripping off material for me' (Hayes, 2005: 8). This means teachers need to have high expectations not only of their students but also of themselves – to model desired behaviour and persist in the face of difficulties (Halpin, 2003). Moreover, teachers can also encourage their students to have high expectations of teachers (Collinson et al., 2000: 29), for example, by using a weekly questionnaire asking students not only to reflect on what they had learnt, but also asking for suggestions on how the teacher could help them learn better.

These teachers work in schools located in disadvantaged communities where all too often it is taken for granted that 'these kids' will never amount to much. They demonstrate the courageous vision (McInerney, 2007) required to defy such accepted beliefs about probabilities among their colleagues and instead focus on possibilities in their students – and in themselves.

Establishing a community of hope

Widespread and enduring improvements in schools can only be achieved through collaboration, within schools, but importantly also more broadly in society (McInerney, 2007). Taking seriously the effect of social and institutional structures on what teachers can achieve means that pedagogy of hope cannot be confined to work by individual teachers. Therefore, Shade (2006: 198) has put forward the idea of 'communities of hope' because 'communities, which weave habits into social customs and institutions, form a vital component of the life of hope'. He points to two responsibilities for members of a community of hope.

First, to implement institutions and policies that are conducive to developing hope. For example, Sarra (2003) worked with the local Aboriginal community to consolidate a school vision. At a national level, it may mean a commitment to educational funding based on principles of social justice, so that all schools have access to necessary resources.

Secondly, a community of hope should support the hopes of all its members. Importantly, this means that everyone, regardless of age, should be recognized as a member who can contribute to the community, not simply be a passive recipient of its benevolence. The resiliency literature agrees that opportunities for active and meaningful participation by young people in their communities are beneficial (Benard, 2004). School students dislike being treated like 'a little kid' (te Riele, 2006b). In contrast, strategies for genuine participation can give young people a sense of being valued as responsible members of the school or local community.

In project A, much of the sense of responsibility and ownership that students feel towards the school comes from their contribution to the physical environment. Displays of awards and achievements, the gardens, outdoor classroom, rainbow serpent sculpture, chicken shed and picnic tables all mean that student contributions to the school community are highly visible. One student was pleased to show off:

> Take a look around, all the gardens and stuff. I'm one of them that put that in, the landscaping crew. A couple of my mates did it with me, done all the gardens and stuff, laid all the turf. Last year there were no plants, no grass, no nothing, just all rocks. Rocks, dirt and mud. Now, you know, it's looking alright out there. (Project A)

The pride students feel is almost tangible – their commitment to the school is valued by themselves and by the school, and that means they want to belong, participate and be successful.

Hope is fundamentally social (Godfrey, 1987) and community is thus an important part of the pedagogy of hope. An early philosopher of hope argued that hope 'is only possible at the level of the *us* ... and does not exist on the level of the solitary ego' (Marcel, 1951, in Halpin, 2003: 16, original emphasis). Moreover, Rorty (in Sanders, 2007) points to the importance of hopeful imaginings for achieving solidarity and institutional reform. The hope an individual teacher has for his or her students is vital, but it is limited if not accompanied by broader social hope and reform.

Critical reflection

Finally, to ensure that pedagogy of hope takes seriously that not all hope is necessarily good or sound, it must include critical reflection. Within the classroom, this includes teachers supporting students to reflect on the effect of their hopes on the well-being of others. Biesta (2006: 281, original emphasis) argues that 'teachers who want to bring hope to the classroom have a task, not only in *supporting* their students' hopes but also in *questioning* and *interrupting* them'. Teachers can help students to reflect on the soundness of their own and others' hopes, and to consider how their hopes may impact on those of others. At the level of the school, critical reflection helps teachers to determine whether/how the school environment itself contributes to student failure. By questioning common practices and suggesting other practices which may be worth trying, critical reflection contributes to more hopeful pedagogies in schools.

At a broader social scale, Rorty (1999) suggests that a philosophy of hope ultimately aims to create a fairer and more democratic society. Sound hope is inherently social – it is not just about myself, but also what is good for my community, my society, the world. Beyond the classroom, critical reflection forms the basis for discussion of 'those principles of procedure and action plans that contribute to the creation of a more equal and more democratic education system and society' (Halpin, 2003: 5). Fostering such critical thinking enables the kind of politics of 'educated hope' that Giroux (2003: 100) suggests will assist 'linking individual responsibility with a progressive sense of social agency'. Critical reflection is thus a key element of the pedagogy of hope, making a contribution to the ongoing and gradual social reform of schooling which can benefit all young people – and society.

Conclusion

The pedagogy of hope is not about putting on rose-coloured glasses, ignoring difficulties or blaming teachers or schools if they are not always successful. It recognizes not only the importance of the agency of teachers but also takes seriously the complex barriers created by social and institutional structures. A realistic but radical politics of hope (Rorty, 1999) needs to replace both naive, unattainable wishful thinking and the all-too-common negative perceptions of certain schools and certain young people in society.

While teachers cannot make all the difference on their own, they can apply their agency through 'learned hopefulness'. As Halpin (2003: 27) explains, 'hope can be mediated – perhaps even taught – within the educational context via the adoption of cultures of learning that accentuate the positive rather than the negative'. Encouraging teachers to take up this pedagogy of hope is not intended to add another burden to teachers' work, but instead aims to provide resources that can help teachers deal with challenging circumstances. Table 8.1 provides a summary of these resources.

Table 8.1 Resources for a pedagogy of hope

A positive culture of learning	Adopt cultures of learning that accentuate the positive Celebrate a wide range of accomplishments, effort, improvement and community spirit Use your creative imagination to locate strengths in young people
Focusing on possibility	Focus on possibility rather than (statistical) probability Have high expectations of your students Have high expectations of yourself Support a school-wide ethos around possibility Courageously reject deficit beliefs
Establishing a community of hope	Implement policies that are conducive to developing hope Build bridges between schools and community Lobby for educational funding based on social justice Support the hopes of all members of the community, including those of young people Create genuine opportunities for active and meaningful participation by young people in their communities
Critical reflection	Reflect whether an alternative hoped-for situation is really better Support students to consider the effect of their hopes on the well-being of others Question common practices and explore new approaches Reflect how to contribute to a fairer and more democratic society

Hope – complex, attainable, sound hope – is a tool for exploring a politics of possibility (Giroux, 2003) in education. Rather than merely critiquing existing practices, this requires the ability to imagine an alternative future. Williams expressed it as follows:

> It is only in a shared belief and insistence that there are practical alternatives that the balance of forces and chances begins to alter. Once the inevitabilities are challenged, we begin gathering our resources for a journey of hope. If there are no easy answers, there are still available and discoverable hard answers, and it is these that we can learn to make and share. (1983, in Halpin, 2003: 127)

This chapter has attempted to make a contribution to such answers, through the pedagogy of hope. Importantly, all teachers, youth workers, parents, and (of course) young people can work together to discover other answers that provide relevant hope for their own context.

Discussion questions

1. Think of a teacher who believed in you. What effect did that have on you?
2. What is the difference between holding on to false (unattainable) hope and having high expectations?
3. How can teachers help build a community of hope, both within their own classroom and more broadly?
4. What taken-for-granted practices have you come across in schools? How could these be changed?

Further reading

Collinson, V., Killeavy, M. and Stephenson, H. (2000) 'Hope as a factor in teachers' thinking and classroom practice', in C. Day and D. van Veen (eds), *Educational Research in Europe Yearbook 2000*. Leuven: Garant. pp. 21–35.

Halpin, D. (2003) *Hope and Education. The Role of the Utopian Imagination*. London: Routledge Falmer.

Websites

Coaching for Hope (UK): http://www.coachingforhope.org/about_cfh/about_cfh.htm

Dusseldorp Skills Forum (Australia): http://www.dsf.org.au/

National Resilience Resource Center (USA): http://www.cce.umn.edu/nrrc/

Note

1. See http://kids.niehs.nih.gov/lyrics/headsh.htm

9 Engaging disaffected young people

Linda Milbourne

This chapter explores:

- alternative pedagogical approaches, drawing on studies of UK community education providers;
- values and ideologies underpinning learning communities working with disengaged young people; and
- challenges involved in sustaining effective alternatives.

Nineteenth- and twentieth-century Europe and America offer many examples of community-based, voluntary endeavours to generate educational alternatives, from working-class community and progressive schools developed from the 1900s onwards (Shotton, 1993), to the urban free school movement of the late 1960s (Wright, 1989), and radical education projects worldwide (Graham-Brown, 1996). Many aimed to create relevant and less prescriptive education in poor communities.

Few lessons from such developments or from recent alternatives inform pedagogic debate, despite a resurgence of approaches challenging formal schooling (Carnie, 2003). This absence is surprising when non-profit organizations have gained new importance in undertaking a growing share of welfare delivery, including initiatives prioritizing the inclusion of marginal young people (Colley et al., 2007). By exploring recent examples of community-based educational organizations offering alternatives to disengaged young people, this chapter seeks to redress a small part of this research gap.

Policy and disengaged young people

Recent policy changes in the UK, as elsewhere, have generated renewed public and academic interest in community-based work and its potential for engaging disaffected young people. Policies concerned with young people have given recent prominence to inter-agency working (DfES, 2006) and securing young people's participation in structured and voluntary activities (DCSF, 2008a).

The British state is obliged to ensure education for all young people, in school or 'otherwise', which is now part of a broader social inclusion agenda, with educational achievement highlighted as a means to preventing future exclusion (DfES, 2004). Policy has ostensibly prioritized 'inclusion', while many initiatives intended to reduce school absence and exclusion have been delivered through off-site projects (Atkinson et al., 2004) involving non-profit agencies. However, community efforts focused on young people outside formal schooling are often undermined by mainstream agency structures and targeted outcomes (Milbourne, 2009).

Conflicting strategies involving tighter regulation of young people and encouraging their participation are evident in recent policy. The negative characterization of groups of young people, fuelled by media hyperbole, is familiar, and has encouraged policy-makers to intensify their surveillance (Muncie, 2006). Recent policy (DCSF, 2008a: 2) underlines redressing this 'unrelentingly negative' view of youth but other policies promote punitive measures. Studies of different professional settings identify an overall shift, from the 1970s, towards increased regulation of young people (Fielding, 2001; Roche et al., 2006). Consequently, altruistic aims in extending opportunities coexist with interventions which monitor and constrain young people's behaviour, problematizing alternative behaviours, and pressuring young people and professionals to conform to prescribed activities and outcomes (Griffin, 2006).

Over successive generations young people's deferred access to economic independence has increased frustration, especially among those with poor expectations of schooling. Coupled with a narrowed, attainment-led school curriculum (Ball, 2001), growing constraints have produced detrimental consequences for young people at the margins of school and society (Cullingford and Oliver, 2001). Recent proposals to extend the compulsory schooling age and the use of school exclusion continue trends visible in the 1990s' truancy sweeps, the 2003 Anti-Social Behaviour Act and increased use of custodial youth justice over the past 10 years (Solomon and Garside, 2008), exacerbating young people's frustrations.

In contrast, the United Nations Convention on the Rights of the Child (1989, Article 12) has prompted worldwide activity around young people's voice. Policy reforms affecting schools and young people's services, including citizenship curriculum, school and youth councils (DfES, 2006) emphasize youth participation and volunteering as components of policy discourse on inclusion and, more recently, social cohesion. Outcomes expressed in terms of 'empowering young people' and 'removing barriers' to accessing opportunities (DCSF, 2008a: 2) are hard to reconcile with strategies outlined above.

Non-profit sector and change

The UK non-profit sector has a history of contributing to humanitarian social welfare which considerably pre-dates public services (Kendall, 2003), providing education projects, advocacy and enabling access to other social institutions (Kruger, 1993). Over two decades, both public and non-profit sectors have changed substantially, transforming roles and inter-sector relationships (Harris and Rochester, 2001). The emphasis is now on pluralism in service delivery, with non-state providers competing for state-controlled contracts. However, as with youth policies, there are inherent contradictions. While much recent policy acknowledges the expertise of non-profit organizations in tackling social exclusion (OTS, 2007), offering powerful legitimation, managerial and performance cultures pervading the sector have generated a markedly different organizational environment (Kendall, 2003).

During the 1960s and 1970s, progressive social movements had a greater impact on community sector values than parallel state services; and community-based education projects typically integrated education with community concerns, fostering more equal, less formal, relationships between learners and tutors (Wright, 1989). Despite isomorphic organizational pressures (DiMaggio and Powell, 1983), many non-profit organizations have carried this legacy of values forward through multiple changes (Billis, 2001).

Crossroads, Horizons and ThePlace: three case studies

The chapter now turns to a study of three long-standing, community-based organizations working with disengaged young people, exploring how their alternative approaches contributed to engaging young people in learning and made a difference in their lives. The detail of such case studies reveals wider lessons for culture and practices in educational work (see Stake, 2000).

The three education projects: Crossroads, Horizons and ThePlace, are small, non-profit organizations, each with a 30-year history. They primarily cater for 14- to 16-year-olds poorly served by statutory provision, and have often taken a critical stance towards mainstream institutions, including through advocacy and campaigning.

The organizations are located in Rushley,[1] an ethnically diverse, impoverished, inner-city area, where some neighbourhoods are among the most deprived in England (DETR, 2000), with 70 per cent of households in social housing, and high unemployment, especially among young people. More affluent parents have routinely selected secondary education and fee-paying schools in neighbouring areas, leaving disproportionate numbers of pupils with special educational needs and eligible for free school meals in Rushley schools, adversely affecting school achievements and reputations. Levels of school exclusion were high, at 25 per cent above national figures.

At the start of the research Crossroads, Horizons and ThePlace were the only non-profit organizations in Rushley offering full-time education for young people out of school, providing 65 places. The organizations had a positive reputation locally for successful work with young people, some of whom had been outside formal schooling for over a year. They received good local and national inspection reports, the latter commending them for 'high quality, successful and cost-effective work'.

A range of staff, supported by volunteers, worked with young people, including teachers and youth workers, several with additional specialist qualifications. Staff met across the projects to share practice and maintained good networks with other local professionals, such as careers, child health, educational welfare and psychology teams, who ran sessions at the projects.

Many young people at the projects had experienced successive school exclusions and referrals between agencies; others were missing from institutional records. Many had poor levels of academic achievement, frequently resulting from long absences from schooling. Fifty-five per cent of the students were young black men, predominantly African-Caribbean and dual heritage, groups with poor records of local education participation. Existing social, racial and economic disadvantages were often exacerbated by other disturbing events, such as placement in residential care; bullying; experiences of violence or mental illness; family drug or alcohol abuse; and unacknowledged learning disabilities. Consequently, experiences of frustration, difference and being poorly valued at school often grew into dissent or opting out altogether, sometimes culminating in aggressive or criminal behaviour.

In what follows, observations and illustrative quotes from staff and young people are used to explore organizational values and practices to, and examine the effectiveness of alternative approaches. Other themes highlighting difficulties posed by changing policy and organizational arrangements are discussed elsewhere (Milbourne, 2002), and the stories of two young people feature in the Case study 10.2 in Chapter 10.

Distinctive alternatives to schooling?

The organizations shared similar goals, offering 'flexibility in addressing students' individual learning needs in a friendly and informal setting' (ThePlace, mission statement). They aimed to 'encourage independence and self-esteem, and empower young people in making positive choices' (Crossroads, mission statement). Lave and Wenger's (1991) analysis of learning as participation in the social world is valuable in conceptualizing approaches to which staff were committed. They emphasized the importance of providing a stimulating environment, promoting social as well as educational development, and making learning accessible to young people with often markedly different abilities and rates of progress. Flexibility was crucial but, as Sonia underlined, it had to *feel* different from mainstream schools: 'I mean, otherwise why bother, you know, a second chance doesn't mean another bite of the same ... Because that wasn't any good for whatever reason ... what could we do that would be different?' (Sonia, coordinator, ThePlace).

Most young people appreciated the small size of the projects, allowing staff to work with groups of six to eight and give individual attention, including negotiating and reviewing individual learning and behaviour goals. The smallness of organizations and learning groups also fostered an informal and flexible ethos, markedly different from most schools. Students viewed it as 'better because ... You just concentrate more ...' (Connor, Crossroads); 'people listen to what you say, not laugh at you', (Cheryl, ThePlace). Young people with previously negative learner identities (Wexler, 1992) were motivated by enjoying activities and recognizing achievements, instead of experiencing boredom or frustration in classes poorly tailored to their needs or interests.

Framing the curriculum: tensions in motivation

Superficially each organization's curriculum overlapped considerably with schools, providing accreditation in core National Curriculum subjects; personal, social and health education; vocational education and careers guidance. Other schemes, involving sports, community activities and group work, enabled most young people to access awards.

However, the approach was different and young people had considerable choice, including varied optional and practical activities; and they defined their own pace and focus of study. Negotiating individualized timetables helped them believe they mattered, generating a mutually more responsive environment. Emphasis on students' prior experiences significantly outweighed targeted curriculum and knowledge transmission; and students had flexible access to facilities and equipment. 'They're learning skills but they can make things for themselves, their friends or family', (Neil, tutor, ThePlace).

By contrast with conventional schooling, activities involved discussion sessions on topics students identified, generating important spaces for them to influence changes to curriculum and rules. When tensions occurred, there was flexibility to take time out, and tutors often worked through problems individually. Practical classes – drama, art, photography, graphic design and woodwork – were also contexts for social and emotional development, and contributed to integrated education projects.

The emphasis on informal learning also involved young people in planning and cooking lunches, which staff and students usually ate together, giving further opportunities for informal discussion. There was also flexible time, when young people played pool, table tennis or computer games, or relaxed in common room or garden areas. There were regular outings and annual residentials, for example, at an outward-bound centre, providing opportunities to experience new activities and build cooperation and trust. Funding contracts prioritized National Curriculum targets and periodically specified other activities. However, achieving the right balance between formal curriculum and activities which would motivate young people proved challenging for staff. Young people were often ambivalent about formal curricula, recognizing the external prestige of learning achievements as an important counterbalance to 'ending up with nothing' (Ian, ThePlace). However, their negative prior experiences reinforced expectations of failure, and competing values and needs often risked undermining their aspirations.

Many young people stressed less tangible benefits from being at the projects. Becky, a victim of school bullying, identified her experience as life-changing: 'They showed me I could be somebody … It give me a sense of myself, when I thought there wasn't nut'ing for me' (Becky, Crossroads). Discussing motivation to attend, Alvin (Horizons), who rarely attended school, reflected, 'Now, I really enjoy it … I never thought I'd do that, look forward to going out come morning'.

Art, woodwork and photography gave some young people ways of expressing difficult feelings, and others routes to engagement. Guy (Horizons), arrested for joyriding, declared, 'I don't know why I bother to come, only for woodwork', but seven months later, admitted, 'I have matured because Greg [carpentry tutor] puts me to the test like, he trusts me'. Gaining young people's trust and offering them trust were key factors in their engagement.

Belonging and respect

Organizational culture was crucial in underpinning pedagogic approaches, and involved fostering young people's sense of belonging. They explained this in different ways, including 'fitting in' and 'feeling comfortable' (Ben, see Case study 10.2 in

Chapter 10), with many young people developing loyalty to the organizations and facilities. If they could feel a sense of ownership, young people had something to value, in turn, helping them to value themselves. 'Then they ... engage in a way that's less defensive, more part of the group' (Alison, tutor, ThePlace).

The projects also functioned as a refuge, both physical and emotional: spaces where young people could feel safe from external threats, whether from other young people, different agencies or adverse circumstances. Acknowledging young people's vulnerability, Pennie (Crossroads tutor) stressed, 'security comes first, before they can focus on learning'.

Young people who had felt devalued as school learners, described how the projects offered a caring environment and a place where they felt accepted. Sonia, explaining her approach to students, stressed, 'Here, we are bothered and, if you're serious, you'll be bothered too. Then we'll ... walk with you as far as we can' (Sonia, coordinator, ThePlace). Students repeatedly identified being listened to, valued and respected as reasons for engaging in the life of the organizations when they had previously rejected schooling. Ashley highlighted this combination as what worked for her:

> They didn't look down on you, they had time for you, they listened. If you had a problem, you could take them aside and they'd help. They treated you like a grown up, and if you're out of order, you knew it ... It really changed how I see things. (Ashley, ThePlace)

Vivica highlighted the culture of respect, and staff believing in her, as distinguishing ThePlace from her experiences of other professional contexts: 'I suppose they really want us to achieve something and that's the first time someone ... like in school or social workers ... really thought I could' (Vivica, ThePlace).

However, barriers to young people's sense of belonging also emerged from the diversity of cultural identities. Peer pressure exerted through racialized and gendered differences (Hayton, 1999), together with disparate abilities, could contribute to experiences of insecurity and, sometimes, continued disengagement. Staff were sensitive to issues arising from cultural diversities and discussed referrals to avoid girls or students from particular ethnic groups being isolated. Early in the study period, staff were predominantly white and female, but efforts to increase diversity resulted in more black and male staff.

As small organizations, members worked together closely generating shared ideas and values, so that changes and developments were often integral to, and grew from, collective working practices. Organizational cultures of this kind are likely to strengthen 'communities of practice' (Lave and Wenger, 1991) through which staff make sense of their work. The longevity of the organizations and long-standing involvement of some board members and staff played a part in the cohesiveness of values and approaches understood and enacted. The learning experiences, engagement, successes and resistances of students also contributed to reinforcing, as well as reassessing and developing, approaches.

Power to influence?

While most students accepted the need for rules and were often self-critical, they also criticized staff; and several staff–student discussions ensued on the boundaries for negotiable space around behaviour, rules and curricula. Often small adjustments resulted, sometimes more substantial changes. However, externally imposed directives, including stringent attendance and performance targets, periodically compressed space for negotiation. For example, coercive placement at Horizons for Keisha (see Case study 10.2 in Chapter 10), as the only alternative to a custodial centre, initially exacerbated her resentments.

When young people felt their views were discounted or rules unfair, they were more likely to retreat into negative behaviour patterns, especially if they felt excluded from influence. However, if their voices were heard and action agreed, negative trends could be reversed. The staff's willingness to use their greater power to renegotiate the barriers inhibiting students' constructive participation often avoided challenging incidents becoming damaging to individuals and the group, which Munn and Lloyd (2005) identify as recurrent elsewhere. Finding the right balance was difficult: roles and boundaries needed to be simultaneously flexible and unambiguous for students. Staff could not readily fall back on pre-described professional roles and approaches and at the same time retain a responsive culture. As Debbie, the Horizons' coordinator explained, it required 'an open mindset about working practices', demanding particular qualities from staff.

Learning processes which influence change in surrounding conditions (whether in curriculum, organizational rules or professional practice) raise questions about differential power, not only between tutors and students, but also between students. When staff relinquish or share power with inclusive aims, they can inadvertently favour more powerful or articulate students and silence others. Staff highlighted these challenges when students redesigned programme activities at Horizons, pointing to a need to protect space for less confident young people, who could otherwise find proposals dominated by more articulate students. Nonetheless, young people understanding how to use their collective power to construct positive changes illustrates the potential for education to develop critical consciousness (Freire, 1974).

Alternatives against the odds

The chapter has explored the distinctive approaches of three non-profit alternatives in engaging young people 'against the odds'. These 'odds' included young people's damaging educational and life experiences which presented significant barriers to institutional participation, and the constraining impact of public policies. Community-based organizations have been applauded for their expertise in tackling social problems but state insistence on performance measures and approaches, which replicate mainstream services, ignores the challenges of such work and the diverse ways in which such organizations have succeeded. As the cases illustrate, dominant institutional demands restrict the space for negotiation with young people, a flexibility at the heart of their practices. What moved young people to engage or to perceive that these organizations offered something different? Pedagogic processes are not separable from the social construction of the learning environment, and whether or not they achieved re-inclusion in conventional institutions, most young people acknowledged their time at the projects as better enabling them to face difficult futures. A culture of respect, security and relationships of trust were crucial in making their learning experiences worthwhile, and distinguished these projects from their previous experiences of schooling.

Underlying these projects' approaches are a more expansive pedagogy and institutional culture than are visible in conventional schooling. Such work requires conceptualizing the goals and purposes of learning beyond the narrow objectives of targets, examinations and knowledge transmission, to broader aims embedded in social experience and organizational practices. Methods which allow students greater control over activities, and encourage problem-solving and group work reflect theories which understand learning as a dialectical process, integrating experience and concepts, observations and action (Kolb, 1984). Such learning results from a balance between learners' ideas and experience, and their accommodating those of others, necessarily reducing power invested in professional roles.

Policy has championed young people's inclusion but these projects' successes with disengaged young people were largely achieved *despite*, not *because of*, external initiatives. Sustaining cohesive values and approaches over time while continually facing challenging conditions points to the strength of the projects' underlying cultures, enabling them to reinvent their practice while accommodating external demands for conventional pedagogy and outcomes. Simply identifying the organizations' communal strengths, as ways in which they sustained their alternative approaches, fails to account for the complex ways in which they secured and maintained their cohesion. Similarly, theories of resistance (Giroux, 1983; Willis, 1977) offer insufficient explanation for patterns of resistance entwined with accommodation, which characterized these organizations. Creating an ethos where staff and young people felt they belonged was crucial in sustaining the organizations' resistance to external pressures, but their willingness to develop and adapt illustrates their resilience in facing and resolving changing circumstances. Their ability to accommodate changes while maintaining the core values under-pinning their organizational meanings marks a distinguishing feature of their successful survival.

There is also a process of continual in-organizational development as newcom-ers join close-knit communities. If organizations aim to engage reluctant learners, they must enable newcomers, initially peripheral, to become insiders. Lave and Wenger (1991) describe the assimilation of newcomers into a learning community as requiring little change from insiders. Here, young people (and new staff) enter-ing the projects brought diverse attitudes and biographies: dispositions (Bourdieu, 1977) which influenced practices, just as the communities shaped them, through their growing involvement. This dialectic explains a crucial difference between these organizations and larger institutional contexts, where structures, rules, pro-cedures and cultures remain resistant to shaping from young people, perpetuating marginalization. (For further discussion of power and dominant cultures, and the role of agency, see Foucault, 1977 and Bourdieu, 1992.)

These organizations have reduced the risks of young people continuing damaging behaviours, not through partial goals of reintegration into unproblematized institutions, but by seeking to understand and work with their perspectives. Their approaches demonstrate the importance of working with, rather than deciding for, disengaged young people; of generating their cooperation towards positive outcomes over time, rather than imposing expedient interventions. Thus the chapter argues the need to resist narrow, conformist and individualized concepts of learning and attainment, which largely discount factors in the social and economic environment contributing to educational exclusion. Conversely, cases here underline the importance of addressing the contexts and practices that exclude, of viewing young people as social actors able to shape their worlds and of exploring pedagogic practices within cultures of respect. By continuing to devise ways of negotiating with young people despite limited autonomies, these organizations engaged with the tensions and possibilities of participatory education, with its related value for wider social participation (Mayo, 1997). Such possibilities offered greater empowerment for young people, demonstrating how such ethos can foster greater effort, commitment and social responsibility, providing spaces for young people to repair damaged self-esteem. These cases illustrate the potential for change through alternative approaches, demonstrating the need for the continued (or renewed) autonomy of such organizations.

Enhancing cultures and practices in small, potentially marginalized provision is insufficient if their wider educative and socio-political approaches continue to be sidelined. Despite these organizations' evident success with disengaged young people, this is yet to be reflected in local or national strategies or wider pedagogic practice. The varied approaches to work with disengaged young people advocated at different times highlight the need for openness to diversity in the present. Exploring not just 'what works' but what inhibits participation, this chapter argues the importance of understanding the complexity of issues and challenges involved in effective work with disengaged young people.

These organizational settings are specific but their resilience in sustaining alternative educational values and organizational meanings 'against the odds' of dominant institutional cultures and pedagogies offers lessons for educational policy and practice. It also generates hope for wider recognition and cultivation of the value of pedagogic diversity, so that we can engage, rather than further exclude, young people disaffected from schooling.

Discussion questions

1. Consider how approaches adopted by the community organizations examined here accommodate or challenge conventional pedagogic practices.
2. Ethos is identified here as distinctive in underpinning pedagogy. How might organizational cultures contribute to engaging or excluding marginal young people?
3. The chapter considers concepts of diversity and differential power related to pedagogic practices and interorganizational relationships. Discuss what insights these offer for other contexts.
4. In a political climate which now emphasizes young people's voice, participation and inclusion, how do examples here offer lessons for the wider context of schooling?

Further reading

Barry, M. (2005) *Youth Policy and Social Inclusion: Critical Debates with Young People.* London: Routledge.

Kehily, J. (2007) *Understanding Youth: Perspectives, Identities and Practices.* Maidenhead: Open University Press.

Levitas, R. (2005) *The Inclusive Society? Social Exclusion and New Labour.* Basingstoke: Palgrave.

Tisdall, K., Davis, J., Hill, M. and Prout, A. (2006) *Children, Young People and Social Inclusion. Participation for What?* Bristol: Policy Press.

Note

1. All names and places are pseudonyms. Information here is drawn from local and regional statistical data.

10 Doing pedagogy differently in practice

Jann Eason (Case study 10.1)

Linda Milbourne (Case study 10.2)

As argued in Chapter 1, the much broader range of young people who now are expected to participate in senior secondary schooling requires renewed consideration of pedagogical approaches. Chapters 7, 8 and 9 have outlined some of these considerations from a research perspective.

This chapter complements those discussions through two practical case studies that demonstrate how pedagogy can be done differently in practice. The first case study is provided by Jann Eason, principal of a vocational, 'second chance' school in Australia. The second case study, by Linda Milbourne, extends her work in Chapter 9.

Case study 10.1 Dare to dream

Jann Eason, Macleay Vocational College, Australia

Located in Kempsey, a regional town 420 km north of Sydney, Macleay Vocational College (MVC) was established in 2001 as a non-government school providing education in Years 9 to 12 for young people who, for whatever reason, would find it hard to stay at a regular high school. A major differentiating factor is the vocational focus, with work placements and vocational certificates integrated alongside the mandatory secondary school curriculum.

Built on a strong foundation of equity, MVC considers that everyone is entitled to a high-quality education, regardless of their background. Student experiences before they came to MVC are not pretty: they may include racially motivated bullying, assaulting police with baseball bats, missing out on breakfast most mornings, sexual relationships from a young age, alcohol and drug abuse, and three generations of unemployment.

Continued

Continued

Kempsey is a relatively disadvantaged area in Australia, and indigenous people are the most disdvantaged. For example, the unemployment rate for indigenous people is 24 per cent in Kempsey (16 per cent for Australia) compared with 11 per cent for non-indigenous people (5 per cent for Australia) (ABS, 2006). Against this backdrop, many Aboriginal parents hope for a better life for their children. Pam's two eldest children ended up moving to MVC – Erin and Conner – but their stories are quite different. Pam explains why Erin wanted to leave her local high school:

> She realized as she was going into Year 9 that a lot of her friends were dropping out and drinking and being on drugs or getting pregnant. So she came home from school one day and she said 'mum I need to get out of here, I don't want to end up like these girls up the road'.

Erin moved to Sydney to complete Year 9 and 10, before coming back home. By then MVC was well established, and Erin decided to go on to Year 11 and 12. Initially Erin was disengaged and her attendance was poor, but she transformed into a responsible and mature student. The most important difference for Erin was the friendliness and helpfulness of teachers. Other students agree: 'It's good when you know the teachers believe in you and they know that you can do it. [...] These teachers actually go out of their way, use their own time to help you.'

This attention means, a local community member argues, that students learn more quickly: '50 per cent of the time in a place like that is probably worth 100 per cent of the time' in a regular high school. Purposefully small class sizes (15 students maximum) support this. Erin was offered one-on-one assistance from the learning support teacher to help her understand and decode assessment tasks. During her final year at MVC Erin was offered a scholarship for a university teaching degree. Deferring for a year to work, Erin will be starting her new study next year.

Pam's second child, Conner, had a more troublesome time as a young teenager than his sister:

> 'Since Year 7, he was in and out of school, getting suspended, wanting to walk out and have a smoke, or not even turn up. Thankfully at MVC they are allowed to have their smoke, instead of running off, they will let them, they have times set aside.'

MVC does not condone smoking, but by taking away its rebellious aura students

Continued

Continued

tend to perceive smoking less heroically, as one student explains: 'They think they're big trying to smoke but people will look at them a lot differently. It's not that you're big […] smoking – you're stupid!'.

Besides being suspended and put on a behaviour programme at his old school, Conner was also truanting. Even if Pam walked him to school herself he would leave again soon after. Moreover, Conner 'has been in and out of trouble with the law'. Pam says that Conner's change since enrolling at MVC (attending school and keeping out of trouble) 'has a lot to do with the teachers, spending time with the students, talking with them'. Teachers explain that taking time is a deliberate strategy to engage students:

> 'These kids won't come to trust the teacher until they actually know you. And so because you've got time to tell them about yourself and have a normal conversation with them, they learn to trust you and then the learning can begin for a lot of these kids.'

Another major strategy is to build on students' interests. Many students, including Conner, enjoy Art, and teachers use this to engage them and help them achieve more broadly. A student who entered MVC in Year 9 with the reading age of a 7-year-old, ended up achieving 77 per cent in the externally marked Year 12 Visual Arts essay. For Conner, teachers are using his interest in computer programmes for making/recording music to build bridges to other knowledge and skills. In particular for boys, it is crucial that education is relevant to their current needs and clearly leads to future employment opportunities, but most importantly be enjoyable, interesting and perceived as fun!

Pam sums up by saying: 'I am so glad MVC is there, I would have had so much trouble with Conner, I just thank them for being there.'

The vocational nature of the college means partnership with local employers is vital. Local businesses provide vouchers of AUS$30–AUS$50 for students who demonstrate good attendance (including telling someone if you are unable to attend work), appropriate dress for work or school, good work (to the best of your ability) and initiative. In the first year these incentives were offered, only three were given out. Last year, MVC in partnership with its local business community realized over AUS$2,000 worth of incentive prizes achieved.

The point is not that MVC makes every student's (or parent's or employer's) dream come true – no school can do that – but MVC does open doors for

Continued

Continued

students, showing them new possibilities. Like the Year 10 boy who became very excited about a thesaurus, saying: 'I didn't even know these words existed!' Or the female student who did a work placement in childcare and ended up travelling to the USA as a nanny. Or the indigenous student who wanted to gain a job based on his merits, not because he is indigenous, and successfully applied for a job as an apprentice cabinetmaker. Whatever it is, the College dares the students to open their eyes to the world and their own abilities, and to get out there and pursue their dreams.

Case study 10.2 Young people at the margins: Ben and Keisha's stories

Linda Milbourne

Ben and Keisha's stories illustrate young people at the margins of UK inner-city institutions. Drawing on data gathered over 18 months, they explore how participation in the community-based project, Horizons, discussed in Chapter 9, made a difference to their futures. Their brevity cannot adequately address the complexity of these individual lives and experiences.

Ben

Ben was 15 when he joined Horizons after missing nearly a year of school and refusing to return. He is white, living on an inner-city housing estate with his mother and older brother. Though positive about earlier schooling, from age 12, Ben's school attendance declined steadily, and by 14 he stopped attending.

School reports and Ben's comments combined to illustrate his gradual disengagement from school, with increasing absence exacerbating feelings of not fitting in. Ben felt frustrated but blamed the poor learning environment rather than teachers' approaches: 'Not, they didn't want to help but we was too many, and people messing about ... too much rough there ... so I just gone off away from it all.' Out of school, in the company of 'friends', he attempted to gain status through trying to steal a mobile: 'It was stupid I know ... from then I got a action plan. They sent me here ... It was kind of a relief yeah'.

Ben identified Horizons' small size and informality as making it easier to learn and gain individual support, in a culture of respect. He also highlighted, 'Not being laughed at, and not needing to pretend what you don't know'.

Continued

Continued

Smallness also made for closer communication between home and education, making unexplained absence harder: 'They talk to … my mum … now she knows more what's going on.' Ben's mother, Pam, appreciated the accessibility of Horizons' staff, commenting on Ben's progress after a few months: 'He's happier now, people aren't bothering him … Before … he was like a square peg in a round hole'.

Ben found discussing concrete changes much easier territory than personal aspects, yet feeling comfortable and belonging were clearly important in developing his confidence and motivation. He was visibly proud of his progress, explaining some differences in Horizons' ethos:

> Now … I'm really learning something, like really understanding … I've learnt more here than I done in three years at Royston [previous school]. My brain is functioning more properly … It's just better. Smaller groups … you can concentrate … on things you want, 'n you got a say … get more help … staff listen. See my folder … It's all what I done this term.

Ben left 16 months later with GCSEs in English, Art and Mathematics, and a Youth Award, having gained a college place for Design Technology.

Keisha

Keisha is African-Caribbean and lived with her mother and siblings in high-rise city housing. She had strong family ties including with her father, a heroin addict. She lived in social care aged 5 and again at 10. Keisha came to Horizons aged 14, after two school exclusions for fighting and a year of missed schooling. Discussing school difficulties, Keisha highlighted lack of respect which often triggered fights: 'The second year I couldn't take … Girls always saying somet'ing to wind you, I can't be in class and learn … You gotta stand up for yourself, your family … That's good about this place, not so many girls … and more respect.'

While out of school, she received a supervision order, after convictions for assault, only avoiding a custodial sentence by agreeing to attend Horizons. Keisha admitted that, despite risking custody, she took months to resolve that she would engage at Horizons. Attempts to re-engage Keisha's interest in education had to acknowledge the drivers for her disengagement – family problems, disputes and care for family members – and had to respect her diverse experiences and responsibilities.

Outside school, Keisha enjoyed working part-time in hairdressing, and

Continued

Continued

valued Horizons' staff supporting her to return there, encouraging her self-esteem. It required staff flexibility and trust, and negotiating an individual timetable which recognized different ways of learning. In return Keisha agreed to attend anger management sessions.

After a chaotic start, six months later, Keisha no longer walked out of Horizons without warning, but sought other ways of handling her frustrations. Keisha explained that respect and 'people … knowing not to pressure me' were reasons she had engaged with learning at Horizons, and highlighted the importance of a flexible culture which allowed her a safe space to 'chill' and work things through. However, home difficulties threatened to undermine her otherwise positive progress.

Keisha received a prize recognizing her first year's progress, proudly acknowledging it was, 'the first time ever, when my mum came, like, to see teachers, it's not trouble'. Several months later, Keisha vanished again, having apparently been turned out of home. She eventually returned tutors' calls, explaining she was pregnant. A small organization like Horizons will continue to track Keisha's case, ensuring that she accesses support for her aspirations in the future.

Albeit two very different young people and outcomes, these examples illustrate common factors in the potential for change through alternative approaches to learning. In Chapter 9, I discuss ways in which the cultural construction of the learning environment underpins pedagogic processes. These examples highlight the importance of an ethos where young people can learn within cultures of respect, with spaces to develop, shielded from bullying and some of the damaging aspects of their lives. Respect, belonging, feeling individually valued and having influence over activities were more significant in motivating Ben and Keisha than conventional attainment outcomes. Constructing such learning spaces depends on a flexibility, responsiveness and recognition of young people's wider experiences rarely feasible in contemporary schooling.

Whether or not they managed to achieve re-inclusion in conventional institutions, Ben and Keisha learned to face turbulent lives and futures more effectively. They also highlight the precarious nature of young people's engagement, suggesting a need to understand what drives their disengagement and to be willing to continually renegotiate pedagogical content and contexts. To sustain hope of alternative futures for Bens and Keishas, educationalists must remain open to insights from diverse experiences and cultures, and promote creative practices.

11 Learning spaces in educational partnerships

Terri Seddon and Kathleen Ferguson

This chapter considers why partnerships 'do schooling differently'. The chapter:

- identifies different ways of understanding partnerships;

- draws on a series of externally funded partnership projects to illustrate key features of partnerships and the distinctive work practices demanded in partnership work; and

- argues that partnerships create distinctive learning spaces outside familiar, official education stories, scales and relations of power.

Partnerships are an increasingly familiar way of doing education differently. In our case (see Case study 14.1 in Chapter 14) we describe a learning space developed through a local learning and employment network (LLEN) – a partnership in Victoria, Australia. The Labor government introduced these LLENs in 2001 as a means of addressing poor education and employment outcomes amongst 15- to 19-year-olds by building community capacity. They operate on an area basis, linked loosely to local government areas, and mobilize different stakeholders in the local community to support young people. The LLENs persist in 2008 following supportive external evaluations in 2002, 2004 and 2007, and now have another three-year funding agreement to 2010.

About partnerships

Policy agencies and governments have actively promoted the concept of 'multi-agency partnership' since the 1980s. Partnerships are seen to provide room to move in the modernization of welfare states. Reforms have produced models of educational organization that endorse market competition. Yet complex problems often require coordinated responses. Partnerships allow actors in specific locales to develop idiosyncratic ways of coordinating activities and building synergies between interested parties in government, the public and private sectors and civil society (Giguere, 2006). In these partnerships, constituencies 'engage in voluntary, mutually beneficial, innovative relationships' that mobilize their 'resources and competencies' in order to orchestrate activities and decision making towards goals that are valued within the partnership (Copenhagen Centre, 1999).

There are different assessments of these developments. Evaluations of partnerships document positive benefits for young people and increased community capacity in the local area. The LLENs, for instance, have helped to identify particular groups of young people who require targeted support to enable them to complete 12 years of schooling or find employment. These very localized processes have led to initiatives that help young mums, link young people up to employers who are looking for recruits, and support formalized training programmes (LLEN, 2008). Yet commentators often argue against partnerships because they open up education to business interests, raising fears that children are being used for commercial purposes and schooling redirected in pro-business directions (Apple, 1993). They create patterns of inclusion and exclusion (Tett et al., 2003), and lead to education provision that is not fully or securely funded (Power et al., 2005).

Understanding partnerships

Our assessment is that there are three different discussions going on around partnerships. Historical analyses consider the emergence of partnerships over time as an outcome of large-scale politics around the state–education relationship. This perspective highlights winners and losers in education. Spatial analyses look beyond these established relations to see patterns in spatial organization. They ask questions about who inhabits different spaces? Whose voices are heard? What concepts are used to make sense of education? Place-based analyses focus on the terms and conditions that enable and constitute particular partnerships. They provide a way of clarifying the identities, practices and cultures that are significant in doing school differently.

Each of these approaches offers important insights into partnerships. We draw on Australian data to reveal features of partnerships.

A time perspective

For much of the twentieth century Australian schooling was premised upon a partnership between the state and the teaching workforce. This model of centralized bureaucratic-professional education had its roots in nineteenth-century innovations (Seddon, 1995). Governments mobilized and coordinated schooling as a means of nation building. Mass compulsory education 'gentled the masses' that formed alongside industrialization. Schooling did the 'public good'. It supported individual development for work, life and citizenship, and managed the population in ways that encouraged national identification and reduced civil conflict. Schooling created a 'place apart from the world' where people could learn the knowledge, skills and dispositions necessary for adult life in a safe space.

Since the 1960s, governments in Australia and overseas have moved away from this centralized model of government schooling. It began with government endorsement of community involvement in schools (such as school councils in Victoria, Commonwealth Schools Commission). This trend shifted towards economic rationalist policies from the mid-1980s to late 1990s, which endorsed decentralization, corporatization and market reforms in education and training. Subsequently these trends were tempered, but not overturned, by renewed interest in localized economic and social development. Ideas of partnership framed themes: supporting localized problem-solving, innovation through community capacity-building, cross-boundary engagement and inter-agency working.

These historic shifts were from 'government' by large-scale interests (governments, capital and labour) to 'governance' (Jessop, 1998). This privileges smaller-scale, localized interest-group participation in decision making. It creates a political system in which there is considerable cultural diversity and many different decision-making centres that are networked together. There is no sovereign authority but an ordering of multiple actors that are specific to particular policy arenas. This ordering determines the agency and voice of each actor within decision-making processes (Rhodes, 1996).

These trends press education towards a decentred, rather than centred, model. Reconfiguring centralized bureaucratic government education as a decentralized network disrupts the familiar stereotype of schooling as a 'place apart from the world'. Instead, schooling is reconstructed as diverse but interconnected 'learning spaces' that interface with everyday life settings more than before.

From this perspective, partnerships seem like soft marketization in the neo-liberalization of social life. Governments have been captured by market ideologies and capitalist profit imperatives, and 'neo-liberalization' has redistributed wealth and social resources to the wealthy (Harvey, 2005). The fear is that partnerships increase educational inequality, undercut social justice and create new patterns of winners and losers.

A spatial perspective

A spatial perspective questions this narrative of winners and losers arranged along a single axis of educational value. This rereading of education draws attention to diverse voices and valuing in education. It taps into increased everyday sensitivity to difference, and the limitations of universalistic claims, that accompany contemporary social and cultural changes (Ferguson and Seddon, 2007).

Since the 1960s, social interests (parents, community groups, business, teachers and, to some extent, students) have challenged the authority of government to know what counts as valued education. Initiatives like the Commonwealth Schools Commission acknowledged cultural difference and authorized its voice. This cultural pluralization was intensified by economic and cultural globalization, which increased flows of people, capital and images. These changes broaden people's everyday cultural horizons and bring them face to face with identities, practices and cultures that are different from those at more familiar local and national scales.

These spatial effects play out in different ways across countries, local areas, education systems and individual lives. It becomes obvious that everyday life is spatialized. It is framed by different norms, social conventions and inherited traditions and shaped by uneven ecologies, technologies and human capacities. Asking 'what kinds of bodies inhabit this space?' opens up the concept of spatial formation, and raises questions about whose narrative articulates these formations.

A space perspective clarifies thrashed out identities and slippery boundaries that construct social and educational formations. For instance, dominant policy and research narratives tend to privilege national systems, policy frameworks and institutionalized actors. This narrative defines centres relative to dispersed others at the margins (teachers rather than students, schools rather than vocational education courses). This spatial ordering marginalizes and therefore silences counter-voices that exist alongside official discourses. Yet there is nothing natural about this way of narrating education. It is a social convention anchored in everyday social and cultural practices (such as funding frameworks, teacher education). Other spatial apertures are possible. Social movements, particularly the women's movement, have mobilized counter-spatialities to have their work spoken about in ways that do not preclude multiple subjectivities of class, sexuality, ethnicity, disability, and so on.

This spatial approach to education reveals many different learning spaces. Some have familiar names within the official lexicon of vertical governmental control (school, classroom, training programme). Others are located beyond this vertical axis, embedded in the relationships that make up family, community and workplace settings. Official discourse privileges narratives at the national scale. Yet there are also learning spaces being narrated at other scales (local, regional, global, individual). Like moving between a telescope and microscope, learning spaces are revealed at world scales and as localized minutiae.

These learning spaces all have their own identities, practices and cultures. They all create inclusions and exclusions, and winners and losers. A spatial perspective stops us assuming that mainstream education is better or worse than dispersed learning spaces. It forces us to recognize that normative claims (old–new; locked in–innovative) rest on assumptions about spatial ordering. For instance, examining which bodies are in which space, and to what effect, shows that some participants gain from partnerships and moving away from traditional structures of power. Yet these participants are often not the same individuals who thrive under the model of centralized, formal education.

A place perspective

A focus on place provides a way of bringing historical and spatial analysis together by defining a locus of inquiry. 'Place' captures a tangible and grounded point of intersection. It is a space-time where there is a complex network of people, technologies, resources and practices that are mobilized as a node within a globally distributed space (Farrell, 2006).

This perspective recognizes the way social and cultural practices are sedimented over time to structure everyday life. It also sees the diversity of spaces, the way they are narrated, and how they enable and disable agency within vertical, horizontal and multi-scalar relations. It shows partnerships to be particular social and cultural constructions made up of fixed and mobile things that are specific to time and space. The 'identities-entities, the relations "between" them, and the spatiality which is part of them, are all co-constitutive' (Massey, 2005: 10).

In the next section we use this perspective on place to consider the terms and conditions that enable partnerships to do schooling differently. We draw on our empirical partnership research to reveal systematic features of partnership learning spaces. These data were generated through interviews with chief executive officers (CEOs), executive officers, administrative assistants and volunteers in 16 LLENs and other partnerships across south-east Australia between 2001 and 2006. We also illustrate these features of partnership through self-reflections on learning in partnership in the course of the Crosslife project (see Websites at the end of this chapter). This was a six-country partnership (Finland, the UK, Switzerland, Malta, Denmark and Australia) in which Seddon was the Australian partner and was appointed coordinator in March 2007. This participant perspective in an international partnership provides further insights into the work required to 'do school differently'.

Doing partnership work
Negotiating relationships

Partnerships constitute spaces of interdependence. They are developed in situations that cannot be addressed either through routine work practices or by one partner working alone. This means that partnerships exist only when partners recognize their interdependence.

The challenge in partnership work is to build alignment between partners. The aim is not to develop solutions to problems but to create terms and conditions that will lead to innovative solutions (for example, by developing new systems and/or designing new institutional arrangements) (Mandell, 2006: 6). It involves negotiating goals and procedures in ways that satisfy all the participating interests. This requires partners to engage with the different ways that partners narrate themselves. If agreement – an agreed narrative – cannot be reached, the partnership does not function.

All partnerships report that a lot of discussion is necessary to develop these ways of working together. Figure 11.1 (based on Seddon and Billett, 2004: 21) captures this complex decision-context.

Partners	**Sponsors**
Establish goals, expectations, ways of working, understandings of performance and definitions of success	Provide resources tied to realization of sponsor's goals. Monetary resources tied to explicit performance outcomes; non-commodified resources (e.g. care, time, gifts) tied to implicit normative expectations of success

Auspicer
Hosts the partnership and provides a location for its operations. Contributes to shaping partnership through explicit negotiation and through the implicit impact of the prevailing culture within the host location

Figure 11.1 The complex decision-context for partnerships

The partners are under particular pressure within these negotiations. They are the front-line actors in the negotiation. They have to reach agreement between themselves, accommodate the requirements and constraints of sponsors and auspicers, and respect the community they serve. In the LLEN this is the local area-based community and its young people. In Crosslife the 'users' were students from different countries who participated in a series of three cross-national workshops. The partners were responsible for mediating the influence of sponsors and host organization relative to the users of the partnership's activities.

This relational complexity is compounded by cultures and traditions, creating non-negotiable inequalities between partners. This was particularly clear in Crosslife, where partners embodied different national cultures and where English was the lingua franca. Yet in every partnership participants are ordered relative to the dominant discourse, for instance, as native or second language speakers, as professionals or as local residents who just care about kids. For example, union representatives on LLEN committees of management commonly reported a sense of being marginalized and of not being sure how to connect and engage with LLEN activities. The LLEN staff also commented on the challenges of building relationships with employers. They noted that it required distinct strategies because employers get frustrated with too much talk, too much committee work and not enough action.

These language issues are not just a matter of communication. They reveal relations of power. This was particularly clear in Crosslife where the use of global English was a direct consequence of global politics (the USA as superpower; the reach of Anglo-corporations like Microsoft; the resistance of Anglo-governments to take language education seriously – the native English-speaking partners were mostly monolingual). In the LLEN these themes were also evident. While people were mostly native English speakers, their different histories meant that they were more or less comfortable with the workings of committees, the training system and government. As partnerships consolidated, some ways of working and talking became a kind of lingua franca – a shared discourse that ordered identities as 'natives' or 'less-than-natives'.

This framing was not just mediated by talk but also sedimented within texts. The character of minutes, for instance, was a source of confusion in Crosslife. Minutes were prepared after each partnership meeting by the planner, a Finn employed to support the project. Yet the minutes recorded the issues discussed rather than the decisions made and actions required, which was the more familiar format for London and Australian partners. It meant that these partners could not really see a record of decisions, whereas Finnish and Swiss partners expressed frustration that discussions seem to go over and over the same ground rather than building on decisions that had been made. In the LLEN, the executive officer generally decided the format for documents, which shaped the culture, priorities and ways of working within the partnership.

Establishing a collective steering and learning capacity

The success of a partnership depends upon constructing an effective steering and learning capacity. This governance framework marks some resolution in negotiation of partners' different ways of narrating themselves and establishes an agreed partnership narrative. It defines agreements, rules and procedures for decision making within the partnership, and mechanisms for reflecting on the partnership with a view to improving its performance. It means that decision making can become routine rather than always requiring negotiation, which is often politically sensitive and demanding in time and emotional labour.

Considine (2006) suggests the following elements of a steering and learning capacity:

- mandate, which encompasses and authorizes shared goals, clearly delineated boundaries, and with clear understandings about the kind of partnership and its ways of working;

- structure, which exists in an organizational and legal form, and makes things happen by realizing the exercise of authority;

- resources, which include a budget and budget process that governs and makes transparent the way resources are acquired and expended;

- activities, which demonstrate the values embedded in the partnership and its commitments, including the gathering and analysis of information to facilitate problem definition, processes and tools for planning, goal setting and decision making;

- impacts, which recognize outcomes of relationship building in terms of capability as a partnership, and also as effects of projects and coordinated actions; and

- outcome indicators, which recognize and provide a basis for monitoring the partnership to inform stakeholders and to reflectively review and improve its activities and ways of working.

When LLENs were established, the government provided a protocol for becoming established. By specifying committee composition and procedures, the government was institutionalizing a governance structure that would enable and authorize the LLENs to make decisions. Accountability focused on compliance with these governance arrangements with some attention to education and employment outcomes for young people.

In Crosslife, there was no pre-specified governance framework. The project proposal defined Crosslife's mandate, but objectives were very embedded in the text. Partners read the proposal in different ways, framed by their own national and institutional cultures and traditions. So there were different views about what the project was trying to achieve. These complexities were compounded by project constraints, including limited funding, institutional cultures of partner universities and the challenge of managing ambitions relative to feasible goals.

Forming a 'partnership space' and identity is fundamental to constructing a steering and learning capacity. This is a negotiated outcome; a narrative framed by the interfacing agencies, their institutionalized cultures and their political ordering. The negotiation of political orders is itself a multi-scalar exercise. Partners operate within one scale (for example, between agencies that were in horizontal or vertical relations to one another) and, simultaneously, across scales (for example, Crosslife was a transnational partnership space, whereas each participating university operated within the national space). Negotiating these relationships bring agencies with quite different attitudes together. Even simple planning conversations involve complex cross-cultural dialogue – tied not just to national or institutional practices but also disciplinary, language, occupational and gender cultures and regimes (Kraus and Sultana, 2008).

Constructing 'partnership spaces' involves distinctive ways of working that build interdependencies. It means coming to terms with different agency narratives and generating an agreed way of storying their partnership. Participants in LLENs talked about 'feeling their way', 'taking up opportunities as they arose' and 'not getting bogged down when things don't work'.

This work was opportunistic but with an eye to the agreed goals of the partnership and the accountabilities related to use of public funds. Opportunities to share views were valued because they generated new insights, a bit like hearing travellers' tales about the world seen from a different place. For instance, discussions at one LLEN revealed public transport to be a major constraint on young people's learning – they could not easily get to school. At another, community agencies revealed that children as young as 10 were saying they wanted to leave school – something schools knew nothing about. Breakfasts were popular as a way of building links with employers because they offered good networking opportunities without being too resource intensive. One LLEN executive officer targeted a particular industry sector and phoned all the employers. Having a chat about the LLEN and about young people in the area was enough to bring a lot of these employers into LLEN processes.

Working together meant overcoming inevitable suspicions that the partnership encroached on established territories. Pre-existing relationships and 'forced marriages' can derail these negotiations, but it is also possible to move through difficulties and work together. As one LLEN noted:

The first six months was spent extinguishing fires among the agendas. Now they can say it was that period. There is the same dynamic now among the membership and the broader community. The principals were new to this and NGOs [non-governmental organizations] and had felt out of the reform process and the region. Now they have found collegial support. Local Government has been impacted too – the municipality has developed a youth strategy and youth officer as a result of the local government rep's role on the Committee of Management. In the beginning, all these people were on the LLEN because they had 'a watching brief', they were watching each other and the LLEN. All feared 'an education take-over'. All have now become energised. We have 6 working parties. All are chaired by Committee of Management members. Participation in the LLEN has increased. Now people want to be involved. (Seddon et al., 2002: 10)

Recognizing and shaping partnership cultural practices to retain an easy openness is important. The location of the partnership is important in this respect because the host organization provides a cultural context that influences partnership operations. Local government hosting embeds the partnership in existing practices of representational and consensual decision making, providing competence in governance but also embedding the partnership in local politics. Hosting within schools provides a foundation for engaging community interests but in ways that tend to be distanced from local politics and wider partnerships beyond education and training. Partnerships located outside established local government and educational networks have to put considerable effort into relationship building and developing capacities for governance.

Fixed-format reporting does not work well with this much diversity. It is important to recognize process outcomes as well as governance and service delivery outcomes (Seddon et al., 2008). These process outcomes include working more closely with partners, sharing information and staff resources, and pooled funding for activities.

Embodying partnership

Success in building a partnership space hinges on cultural work across several dimensions, as outlined in Table 11.1 (based on Billett et al., 2005).

This partnership work builds shared meanings but these only become binding on partners through the responsible use of power. Partnerships mobilize collective agency in order to realize collectively agreed outcomes. Their capacity to achieve outcomes depends upon the political regime that is constructed and the way it is enacted. It is framed by the terms and conditions negotiated between partners, with the sponsor and host organization, and in relation to the wider contexts within which they operate.

Table 11.1 Dimensions of cultural partnership work

Dimension	
Cultural-scoping work	Identify, articulate and conceptualize partnership Reflect, review and revise purposes
Capacity-building work	Share information, successes and strategy. Coordinate activities across partners. Journey together over diverse histories and cultures to build new understandings and capacities for action
Trust-building work	Develop processes and activities that engage, inform and are informed by partners' contribution Expect, welcome and act upon partner input
Connection-building work	Nurture relationships. Create spaces for all voices to be heard Recognize and consolidate existing relationships and contributions. Assess impact on the partner
Collective-working work	Develop infrastructure and resources for governance Develop strong and strategic leadership Promote close relationships among partners

This political regime is different to that existing in a single organization. First, the partners may not be strictly equal but they are in horizontal, rather than vertical (superior–subordinate) relations. Second, the exercise of power depends upon how well participants can build relationships and mobilize them towards preferred outcomes, rather than just on authority based in control of resources or expertise (Mandell, 2006).

Much depends upon the soft skills and emotional labour of participants. Comments from interviews capture the character of this partnership work:

> Our chair was discursive and low key, often drew out different opinions and people were not used to this tabling of their thoughts.

> Take on board the politics of the organizations involved. You need to massage the egos of those who can help … Go in boots and all as one, if there is no progress in four meetings, you will lose the busy ones who are the ones you need.

> Make sure there is conversation which welcomes and gives value to the employers and participants.

Partnership work entails control with a light touch, steering relationships through the 'aesthetics' of situations. Creating a pleasant environment makes people more comfortable and productive. One executive officer described herself as 'like a madam' who 'gets the lighting right, gets candles on the table, and good food' to show partners they were appreciated and valued. They had to understand why they were important to the LLEN but also realize their interdependency in the partnership. She had to help them appreciate each other's contributions to that relationship and also feel as if they were in control. She could not physically make things happen on her own but depended on others in the partnership to realize the LLEN's service to the community.

This cultural work entails an embodiment of partnership. Partners come to demonstrate a distinctive mindset that is open to power sharing and learning. Partnering means having a commitment to the whole collaborative agenda, despite conflicts between partners and partners' organizations. It also means respecting and recognizing partners' equal right to speak, and the need to develop new ways of behaving and dealing with one another.

Learning to work together in these ways is a process of cultural change. It requires time, trust, effort and the establishment of norms of flexibility and reciprocity. This 'netiquette' embraces good communication, respect for others' autonomy, limiting claims on scarce resources (especially time), reciprocity and negotiation, dialogue and conflict resolution (Mandell, 2006: 17).

The weight of learning spaces

What does all this mean for educating young people differently?

The final Crosslife workshop involved tutors and students in a 'walkabout' process of 'learning Malta'. Travelling from walkabout to workshop discussions we moved imperceptibly from national to transnational learning spaces. The difference was stark. Artefacts, like crucifixes on the walls of classrooms, revealed the relations of power that construct and narrate Malta as a learning space. Questions, transgressions, open-ended explorations characterized the workshop. Case study 14.1 in Chapter 14 shows similar, lightly institutionalized, social relations of learning in an LLEN.

Learning in partnership spaces differs from learning spaces within heavily institutionalized national education systems. Moving across scales means moving between frames consolidated through differently configured relations of power. The basso profundo of state–church power within national systems has a different aesthetic to that framed by negotiated partnership power relations.

This light touch frames a lighter, evocative, provocative learning space. It is accompanied by 'lite' resourcing that sheds costs of learning onto individuals and communities. It also sustains learning narratives that are inevitably incomplete and whose contradictions create apertures to see things – voices, bodily effects, emotional labour and processes – that are often invisible in established educational ordering.

Decentred education does not displace power relations. However, reliance on contact, influence, strategic manoeuvre and well-timed promotion suggests that there is more to know about multi-scalar partnerships and the way they 'do education differently'. It also suggests that more reliable and constant modes of centralized funding and curriculum tends to evolve into work practices that are not able to meet the needs of all learners.

Discussion questions

1. What features surprise you about partnership learning spaces?
2. What differences exist in the work practices, work organization and working knowledge in partnership learning spaces and in regular school spaces?
3. What artefacts indicate the character of learning spaces and what do they tell you about its stories, scales and relations of power?
4. What do you need to think about if you work in partnership learning spaces?
5. What challenges do partnership learning spaces present for social justice?

Further reading

Sachs, J. (2003) *The Activist Teaching Profession.* Buckingham: Open University Press.

Veugelers, W. and O'Hair, M. (2005) *Network Learning for Educational Change.* Milton Keynes: Open University.

Websites

Crosslife project, VET and Culture Network: http://www.peda.net/veraja/uta/vetculture/crosslife

Local Learning and Employment Networks: http://www.vsc.vic.gov.au/links

UK partnerships – NFER Excellence in Cities Ed Action Zones: http://www.standards.dfes.gov.uk/learningmentors/downloads/nferEiC.pdf

US partnerships: The Chicago Public Education Fund: http://www.cpef.org/ab_overview.htm

12 E-learning technologies and remote students

Stephen Crump

This chapter aims to:

- outline the findings on a research study into the introduction of interactive distance e-learning for remote and isolated communities in Australia;

- illustrate the ways in which access to interactive distance e-learning has provided unique and innovative opportunities for education and training to individuals and communities from primary school to adult re-entry; and

- reflect on the advantages and disadvantages of interactive distance e-learning as an example of providing hope to geographically disadvantaged individuals and groups, within a complex and testing physical and interpersonal environment.

This chapter will provide a policy and practice analysis of the Interactive E-Learning Distance Education (IDeL) project in rural and remote Australia, a joint undertaking between the Australian government, the governments of New South Wales (NSW) and the Northern Territory (NT) and the information technology (IT) service provider Optus Singtel. In doing so, the chapter will also provide information about the relationships between new technology, the participants and their educational needs, expectations and practices that enable distance education to be done differently and, that data suggests, better.

The chapter addresses the theme of 'place and time' in the way that people educationally disadvantaged by distance are being empowered and enabled to communicate in real time, through satellite-delivered lessons (one-way vision), improved audio and the Internet, with their teacher and each other. The IDeL service is provided to 'School of the Air' (SOTA) students and their families and to remote schools and townships; that is, mostly students and parents on isolated homesteads, students and adults in isolated Aboriginal communities, and to adults seeking vocational education but living on isolated properties or living in small towns. In many cases, these communities experience a range of disadvantages, not just in education but also in public services, employment, health facilities and transport.

That is why education needed to be done differently to the traditional mode of 'paper and post' distance education lessons that were not able to be easily synchronized with student needs, lacked immediacy to the context of rural and isolated students, and were supported by very poor audio quality and unreliable delivery of lessons over radio and/or telephone. Sitting on top of these day-to-day difficulties, the *Australian Social Trends* (ABS, 2008) report indicates that while regional Australia is more educated in 2006 compared with 1996, the outcomes of schooling in remote areas has fallen further behind the cities, with minimal increases in participation in education over that decade. Given the difficulties faced in 'the bush', these findings are not surprising, though they need not continue if schooling is done differently, and better. IDeL, I argue, provides this circuit-breaker.

Since 2003, IDeL has brought new technology and educational services to over 500 users. The expansion of access to education using the technologies available in the digital age is a global trend, not only for rural communities. For isolated learners and communities in the IDeL project, the essence of the change being brought about by the technology is the addition of visual modality, fast (and in some cases initial) access to the resources of the Internet, and the opportunity to control and direct some of their own learning (Crump et al., 2005). In 2007, further expansion saw teenage students and more adult learners brought into the programme in different locations and for different learning experiences, including some from mainstream secondary schools and the expansion of IDeL for vocational education and training. By linking IDeL to video-conferencing and smartboards, the programme is accessible by most school and vocational education and training sites in NSW and increasing numbers in the Northern Territory through the use of 'virtual' studios (satellite delivery from a laptop, not a fixed studio site).

The discussion in this chapter focuses on data which have shown significantly improved access for remote and isolated Australians to quality of learning and teaching for school students and adult learners in regional and remote sites, to variety that has shown new dimensions unachievable through radio and post, and to improved quality and reliability of distance education.

The project has also uncovered improved motivational effects on students from all age groups, socio-economic status and race; how parents and families feel less 'remote' not only for education; how parents feel more confident in supporting their child's learning; and how access to the World Wide Web allows families to stay closely in touch with government initiatives and changes to policies and curriculum, as well as to explore easily and quickly educational issues and research around the world (Anderson, 2008; Crump and Boylan, 2008; Crump et al., 2008; Devlin and Hutchinson, 2009).

The relationship between education and ICT

In 1951, Australian teachers adapted Royal Flying Doctor two-way radio equipment to create a 'School of the Air', with excited reports of 'transceivers' with a range of several hundred miles enabling isolated students to hear their teacher for the first time. This has now been replaced with real-time video, shared computer applications, graphics, audio-conferencing, online chat and email which enables isolated students (and their tutor/parents) to see their teacher during the lesson for the first time.

Extensive research has been conducted into whether new technology adds to, or detracts from, positive outcomes in schooling and for education systems (Crump, 1999). Substantial themes can be summarized as:

- almost anyone/any age group can be taught online, with training and support;
- communities play an important role in e-learning because they provide active social communication and interaction;
- cultural, social and economic influences on the classroom need to be considered and understood for effective use of information and communication technology (ICT) in schooling;
- ICT has become a high budget priority for schools, school systems, further and higher education;
- education policy for ICT is inadequate, inconsistent and anachronistic; and
- digital divides exist within school systems, states and nations, as well as across them.

However, new technologies in distance education have been largely overlooked. One of the earliest critiques asked whether technology was part of the solution or part of the problem (Apple, 1987) and this remains a pertinent question. Nonetheless, teaching practices in distance education are developing with technological innovation, as Finger and Rotolo (2001) argue, with distance education increasingly characterized by different and more interactive teaching and learning strategies made possible by new communication technologies. The development of the Internet is considered as defining the present generation of distance education practice, though it is here that too little is known, especially for small school or home-based learning.

Goodyear (2000) argues that education is one of the last fields to learn the lesson that technology must be designed around a thorough understanding of the needs and 'working practices' of its intended users. In the absence of such knowledge of and from intended users, it is not surprising that poorly designed technology (and software) is a feature of e-learning. Part of the reason that, while the IDeL project offers hope through more and superior options for education and training for remote and isolated Australia, as shown by the clearly identifiable improvements illustrated in this chapter, this hope is tempered by a number of technological and policy tensions between operational and practical expectations and experiences, that is, 'complex hope' (Grace, 1994: 50).

'Opening our eyes'

For our project, 'Opening our eyes', there were three key areas to explore what is happening in satellite delivered distance education, related to student and teacher daily practices and opportunities to access education and training in different and better ways: expanded curriculum (a wider range of subjects/materials/teachers each student interacts with); peer interaction (opportunities for collaborative learning) and connectivity (both literally and feeling more connected with the class, community and rest of the world).

The title for the project came from a comment from a participant, in the pilot study, that IDeL had opened their eyes not only to their teacher and school, but to their community where they lived and to communities in similar and different situations across the globe. This alone is a significant difference, as it triggered a rapid shift in the way many students, families and groups using IDeL began to re-imagine their lives, and rethink their identity (see Crump and Twyford, 2009).

Investigating these areas of change positioned our project to examine the connections between the levels and types of participant experiences, activities and actions in the context of IDeL delivery to remote and isolated communities as well as make comparisons to mainstream schooling. Lack of proximity to a school, college of technical and further education (TAFE) or university can contribute to low participation levels for rural, regional and isolated students who have fewer options to pursue career goals locally, many having to leave for urbanized areas for work or to pursue other interests.

Access to education of an appropriate standard and quality is a significant concern in rural Australia, as distance creates barriers to the provision of, and access to, education and training services (HREOC, 2000). These barriers had been significant, especially for Aboriginal Australians not only because of distance but also because of colour and language in pursuing options for future employment. The

Commission saw the provision of that access as a social justice issue:

> For a number of reasons, Aboriginal people have not participated to any meaningful extent in distance education and School of the Air programs. One reason – and this impacts on the delivery of Indigenous education in general – is that many parents perceive their lack of resources and literacy and numeracy skills as barriers to children's participation in such programmes. (HREOC, 2000: 10)

As this chapter will demonstrate, IDeL has allowed many isolated individuals and communities, black and white, young and older, to more fully participate in education and training.

'School of the Air', distance and open education in Australia

The first SOTA was established at Alice Springs in the Northern Territory of Australia. The IDeL programme began in another iconic institution for rural and isolated education, the Broken Hill School of the Air. Other long-standing elements of rural education in Australia include one-teacher schools, central schools, the country area programme (still current in 2009) and assistance for isolated children, including a boarding allowance and second home assistance. While the advent of being able to do lessons by distance over radio in 1951 was very warmly welcomed, over time the limitations of this technology became more than obvious, with parents who had experienced radio telling us (in 2007):

> The quality of the radio (audio) some days was really good, some days it was not flash and the towers would go down quite regularly. (BHGP1431-Pol)

> It was pretty much a whole bunch of static and a lot of really hard work listening. (BHGP1430-Pol)

The IDeL programme is an unusually large and complex innovation in the field of education and technology. As noted above, innovative technologies that have been incorporated into distance education over time in an attempt to overcome the disadvantage that is associated with isolation and satellite-delivered lessons have been the catalyst for a 'quantum leap' in the quality and quantity of how students, young and old, can participate in learning without having to leave their home or community. This has been an important development because, in the twenty-first century we are a much more visual society, and knowledge has shifted from print to multimedia formats, and has become instantaneous and ephemeral.

Different and better?

The dilemma facing teachers and students when the IDeL project began was how to use all the technology at their finger tips, whether in the distance education studio, or at home or in a remote school, and still focus on learning. Teachers were keen to explore the expansion of the curriculum, and the immediacy of the learning experience allowed through the ICT, but their main concern was for students (young and older) to engage in the lesson rather than just with the technology. Teachers continued to chase that 'teachable moment' in each lesson and, therefore, wanted to feel they were in the room with their students (hundreds of kilometres away) and the technology available through IDeL certainly assisted teachers to grab their students' attention.

Using different technologies also helped teachers increase the scope for structuring the lessons to develop individual progression and/or meeting individual students' needs, and for doing so immediately and appropriately rather than weeks later through posting back a piece of work when the student had, most likely, forgotten what it was all about. The result of having vision and being engaged and interacting in real time was, as one teacher (WIA1448-Pol) put it, that students became 'addicted' to the lessons. In a NSW location, where the satellite was on a trailer to enable lessons to be delivered in very remote schools and for vocational training, so keen were the students to keep learning this way that they removed the wheels so that the trailer could not be driven away and thus deprive them of their lessons.

The IDeL experience is an example of authentic learning, where there is a 'live' feed to the class and it is demonstrably interactive and relational, not didactic or simply transmissional. Teachers report students so engaged that they work hard during satellite-delivered classes and do not necessarily wait their turn (as they had over radio). Authentic learning and quality teaching is demonstrated when there is a *process* of development, thinking, planning, acting and reflecting, with the purpose of the learning embedded in all that is done and visible, as well as intellectually and through reflection. Dabbagh (2005) argues that this type of scenario illustrates a harmonizing of pedagogical models, instructional strategies and learning technologies – what she refers to as situated or distributed cognition.

Alternatively, Siemens (2005) calls this 'connectivism', or learning as network-creation, which fits nicely into the *modus operandi* of 'School of the Air' and IDeL. Learners are now in a learning network weekly, almost daily, compared to two or three times a year during a residential or 'mini-school' held in town under the 'paper and post' regime. Seeing learning as a connection forming process, breaking down perceived differences between literal and abstract knowledge and between personal and physical space and time, provides a means to move forward from seeing learning as simply behavioural, systemic or constructed. This is important for trying to understand the very complex variables in the activities occurring in interactive distance e-learning.

Reshaping vocational education and training

Through IDeL, three TAFE NSW institutes (Western, New England and North Coast) are able to provide vocational education courses (VET) to rural and remote Aboriginal and non-Aboriginal communities. In addition, from 2008, VET courses were offered via IDeL to senior secondary school students in remote towns in western NSW because as one teacher explained, for all these groups:

> they're never going to get good provision of (educational) service out there unless you use technology to get it to them. They can't travel in, it is too far away for them to travel in to the nearest campus. From Bordertown, 480kms one way is a bit much! And there is the cost of petrol, plus you need a big 4 wheel drive. (IPE1450-Pol)

The IDeL satellite project for VET was implemented by the TAFE NSW Outreach and Aboriginal Programs via a partnership between the three institutes, initially utilizing the NSW Department of Education 'School of the Air' and distance education centre studios. Using satellite delivery has allowed notions of minimum class size (normally 15) to be reconceived as, with IDeL, the 'class' can be made up of people from small communities, and individuals in homesteads, members of families travelling for work or pleasure, and people isolated by illness or other problems. Between 2003 and 2005, over 500 of the most isolated people in NSW became TAFE students via satellite, many accessing TAFE for the first time. As one IDeL facilitator explained:

> We've still got many communities and many individuals who aren't within 'cooee' [calling distance] of broadband (ha!) so we really need the satellite to reach those people … and it is a large part of our business, delivering to geographically isolated people (…) or anybody whose access to TAFE is disadvantaged or there are barriers – that's our brief, to reduce those barriers. (IPE1450-Pol)

Studios are located in Bourke, Broken Hill, Casino, Dubbo, Port Macquarie and Walgett in NSW. Rural and remote homesteads on 'School of the Air' programmes, as well as other school and VET sites linked to the network, can receive training delivered over IDeL. As noted above, the TAFE institutes also have a mobile satellite trailer and laptops, which can be taken on a short-term basis to remote locations and log into IDeL studio lessons once the satellite dish is locked on. While the appearance and capability of the technology is an important and necessary precursor to doing schooling differently and better for rural and isolated Australia, the educational philosophy for reaching out to and teaching people, young and older, who are hoping to do schooling and training differently, was just as important, as one VET teacher explained:

> The 'Outreach' model of negotiating the content and the timing of the courses directly with the students has meant that what we've been delivering on satellite is exactly what the students want, rather than Daniella [another teacher] or I deciding what might be a good idea. So that makes it very real and relevant for students. (IPE1450-Pol)

Students receive interactive lessons using specialized software which enables them to see and hear the teacher, hear other students and to receive shared applications that are not directly loaded on their own computer. Teachers are able to hear students, can control what students see and hear, what programmes students have access to, and also which student replies or responds during the lesson. This ensures that all students are involved and participate. The technology also supports an internal mail feature, the ability to share web links, PowerPoint presentations and other documents, as well as a quiz feature. As noted above, the interactivity enabled by satellite delivery has been hailed by many participants (teachers and learners) as providing a generational leap forward in distance education.

According to Sedgers et al. (2005), the range of TAFE courses and subjects that have been successfully adapted for satellite delivery has exceeded what was previously thought possible with even very practical subjects being delivered. Sessions on basic computing, modules that support home tutor training and programmes on building maintenance, tractor maintenance, electronics, Aboriginal cultural practices, hair and beauty, cooking and massage have been delivered successfully over IDeL. Sedgers et al. (2005: para 10) quote a student as reporting:

> The TAFE delivery via satellite is fantastic – making learning possible for us out here. I would not have been able to do this course if not for the satellite. It would have been too hard to get the time in town, baby sitters and organize things on the station too. I would have just fumbled my way through and done things the slow hard way or not at all. (SS1)

This is an exciting project also for teachers (Sedgers et al., 2005: para 12): 'So far it's been a magical experience. These students are so keen, so positive and so grateful – it's a joy to teach them. It makes you feel that you are making a difference to people's lives' (ST1).

Reshaping education and training for Aboriginal Australians

TAFE Outreach programmes in NSW have identified the learning needs of a range of target groups. One of the most effective outcomes from the IDeL innovation is the way satellite technology has provided training to Aboriginal communities. Remote Aboriginal communities utilize both the fixed satellite sites, as well as a satellite dish on a car trailer, to access TAFE training. As one IDeL facilitator explained:

> These learners were isolated and not in contact with TAFE or any training really. They didn't have access at that stage and that was probably the main guide (for starting IDel) with our first remote Aboriginal community with our satellite dish trailer. […] we had good connections with the communities (through access and equity programs) that certainly helped and that led to the outcomes from that of having these Indigenous people successfully learning by distance and using technology. […] And the fact that they would accept you as their teacher and friend and you had not set foot in their community, was astounding really. (IPE1448-Pol)

Another teacher in our research observed, for Aboriginal communities,

> I know they never thought they'd ever be able to do it. But now there is the access, the communications, the networking, just the confidence building and empowering them to use the technology. [IDeL has] helped them see outside their world, outside their own community, and seeing past that a bit more because they actually see other things, even though they are sitting in the comfort and security of their own community. (IPE1448-Pol)

Two Aboriginal students who studied over IDeL to become teacher aides in their own community, in the afternoon after helping out at the local school, told me:

> I think the skills are the important thing, but I guess the qualification is important if you want to move onto somewhere else, anywhere. [The IDeL course] has given us strategies to use in different situations. [Without the course] I guess we may have been able to go into Queensland as it is only 10 kms away, that is a lot closer than Tamworth [300 kms away in NSW], but often things do not happen between states [as they each have different education systems]. […] I would like to say I enjoyed the course and

the conference. I was really happy. That's why I followed through. Me and Melody was the ones that sat through it and kept going all the way to the end. So, thank you [the teachers] also. And we are putting things to use that we got out of the course. (NES1446-Pol)

The IDeL programme has allowed schooling to be done differently for hundreds of individuals and scores of communities that were significantly deprived of access to education and training because of where they live, before satellite delivery was provided. IDeL offers real and tangible hope to these people and communities as they gain qualifications and skills only able to be dreamt of beforehand.

The results are conclusive. For VET delivered over the IDeL infrastructure, out of 417 enrolments (2005) there were 376 completions (90.3 per cent) which is unprecedented for distance education for this context and comparatively high for course completions against mainstream VET classes (Sedgers et al., 2005: table 1). This type of outcome allowed a capacity building within remote communities and within the TAFE system that was not possible through other means and modes of delivery for education and training. Young people, family members, adults and groups within communities have learnt a broad range of skills, not least high levels of ICT competency, as well as gaining a broad range of VET qualifications otherwise unobtainable. In the context of reluctant learners, early school leavers, education handicapped by health issues and inadequate and poor resources, this is a remarkable achievement.

Reflections

The education and training outcomes of the IDeL innovation as outlined in this chapter offer genuine and tangible hope to the thousands of participants, spread across remote areas of Australia that they can participate more fully, more meaningfully and more productively in education and training. But it is hope beset with real difficulties and complexities.

Despite the power of contemporary ICT, the IDeL technology does not always work without a hitch. Finding and maintaining capital and human resources in a large education system with competing demands has been a constant challenge for the IDeL operatives and policy planners in NSW and the NT, as well as in the service provider and at the national level. In remote communities the need for a community coordinator to be trained to be the IDeL contact, motivator, operator and facilitator was something that was only slowly realized, leading to some communities dropping out of the scheme because of initial poor outcomes. Student and teacher expectations have soared, providing further difficulties in trying to meet levels of quality and service that were unimaginable with radio lessons.

So hope is there, but it is tempered by realities imposed by distance, geography and local human capital, and physical and educational resources. But rural and regional Australians are resilient and creative. Drought, bushfires, floods and plagues are part and parcel of everyday existence, so they are no strangers to hope being complicated by practical difficulties and human and government failings. The IDeL project is just one example of where the commitment to make this happen meant that the tyranny of distance was beaten down and overcome.

Discussion questions

1. What is meant by the phrase 'the tyranny of distance'? How does where one live impact on opportunities for education and training, in remote and regional areas as well as metropolitan schools?
2. In what ways does interactive distance e-learning create new ways and means for doing schooling differently?
3. Do you agree with the claim made in this chapter that IDeL not only allows schooling to be done differently, but also to be done 'better'?

Further reading

Christie, M. (2006) 'Local versus global knowledge: a fundamental dilemma in remote education', *Education in Rural Australia*, 16: 27–37.

Fletcher, J., Tobias, S. and Wisher, R. (2007) 'Learning anytime, anywhere: advanced distributed learning and the changing face of education', *Educational Researcher*, 36: 96–102.

McLoughlin, C. (1999) 'Culturally responsive technology use', *British Journal of Educational Technology*, 30: 231–43.

Websites

Dubbo Technology Office in New South Wales: http://dart.det.nsw.edu.au/html/studios.html

International Council for Open and Distance Education (ICDE): http://www.icde.org/

Northern Territory DEET – IDL: http://www.ict.schools.nt.gov.au/idl/index.shtml

13 Part-time schooling

Marie Brennan, Eleanor Ramsay, Alison Mackinnon and Katherine Hodgetts

This chapter explores the policy and practice of part-time senior secondary study in the South Australian context in order to:

- open up questions about what counts as 'normal' senior secondary schooling; and

- demonstrate that young people's lives are complex, such that school and work and many other responsibilities/interests require change in school organization and ordinary expected practice.

The emerging issue of part-time senior secondary study

Australia is now a high-achieving but low-equity educational nation, as McGaw (2006) has noted, considering we have both very high achievement in literacy, mathematics and science in the Organisation for Economic Co-operation and Development (OECD) Programme for International Student Assessment (PISA) tests, and a long tail of poor achievement among Aboriginal, poor and rural/remote students. Most of that tail will not even attempt senior secondary schooling, to gain their (usually two-year) certificate of education marking the end of schooling. In the state of South Australia, retention across all schools is around 65 per cent, making it one of the lowest in the country and a priority policy issue in a poor state with less robust prospects for job growth. There was thus strong interest in a partnership research project investigating part-time study in the senior secondary years, most prevalent nationally in South Australia but about which there is little known in the state or indeed elsewhere. In this chapter, we outline what we have learned about part-time study in examining statistics in South Australia, and in case studies of 14 schools, involving questionnaires of students, interviews with teachers and principals, and focus groups of students. Of course, part-time has long been a feature of elite schools, where the head prefect, or competitive sports team members will take a lower load, or repeat a year in order to contribute differently to the school community. However, once part-time becomes more of a mass phenomenon, it changes its meaning. Our question was whether the option of part-time study for a growing number of students led anywhere or instead was a cul-de-sac, an ineffective holding pattern that might stall attrition but not contribute to successful educational outcomes including completion. Nobody knew.

While some aspects of part-time secondary study are particular to South Australia, there is evidence that this trend is present, and probably growing, across the country. Its longer history in South Australia dates from the early 1990s as extended completion was part of the design of the South Australian Certificate of Education (SACE), enabling it to be undertaken part-time. By 2007 the strict time-limits for secondary certificate completion had been removed or significantly relaxed in all states and territories, making way for (or indeed perhaps reflecting) the trend towards part-time study. It was intriguing therefore that almost nothing was known about which students study part-time, or why, nor about the outcomes of part-time study in terms of retention, engagement and completion.

Defining part-time?

We discovered that there are multiple definitions of full-time (and thus part-time) in use, some based on formal definitions and others on local interpretations. Each institution with whom young people interact seems to have a different definition. The federal government deems full-time to be 75 per cent of load, and this becomes relevant in administering a range of programmes, for example, international student visas, or eligibility for allowances/pensions such as single-parent and disability allowances, travel concessions, job training, Aboriginal away from home allowance, or youth (independent) allowance. The state authority administering the SACE has a different definition of full-time and part-time, counting subject 'load', and there is a complex staffing formula operating from the State Education Department for counting full-time students. Schools themselves interpret each of these definitions locally, making sense of them in the context of their communities and their students' lives. The usual expectation is that full-time is 12 semester subjects in Year 11 and 10 semester subjects in Year 12. However, some students attend school full-time and deem themselves full-time, whatever their subject load, while others with a full load clearly move in and out of their schools or may not even attend school at all, so another definition of part-time is student self-declaration. Sometimes people complete a qualification, for example, a vocational 'Certificate III' and it is entered into their record with SACE after it is completed. And other institutions such as technical and further education (TAFE) can 'claim' students as enrolled in vocational subjects so two institutions report them as 'part-time' and are funded accordingly – but the student is in full-time study!

Such diverse definitions make it hard to 'capture' the population with any clarity. In many of the schools we studied, students themselves could not, for the reasons above, state that they were part-time. Many teachers only knew of the attendance of students in their own subject and did not know their students' overall load. Finally, student attendance and load can change over time, between their enrolment plans and later events that emerge to alter those plans.

Who studies part-time?

Ramsay undertook a statistical analysis (Ramsay, 2005–06) which showed that part-time study, as reported to the State Education Department, was significantly correlated with attendance at educationally disadvantaged schools and concentrated in small number of sites: four adult re-entry schools, an open access college, and a few high schools which were each atypical in other respects. Nevertheless significant numbers of part-time students were also scattered across the state in all kinds of schools, and they outnumbered the highly concentrated group noted above. While older part-time students (20+ years) were more likely to be in Year 11 and the younger ones in Year 12, the younger students were the largest cohort and were spread across nearly a hundred schools in the state.

Significantly, the correlation between high levels of part-time study and educational disadvantage held true irrespective of students' age or year level. Census data indicate part-time senior students' numbers are highest in the Northern Territory, South Australia and Tasmania, each of which have a high proportion of their population in the lowest socio-economic quartile, all suggestive of a relationship between poverty and part-time study.

The extent of part-time study in South Australia

A favoured piece of data from our study was originally developed by our partner, the accreditation and assessment authority (SSABSA, 2006) for the review of the SACE which occurred during the time of this study. An astonishing 69 different enrolment patterns were identified across all students commencing in 2000 across a four-year period (see Table 13.1). One of our most interesting tasks has been to unpack what these patterns meant in practice, especially the mysterious 59 different patterns aggregated in the last line.

The first two lines of Table 13.1 indicate the numbers of full-time 'traditional/normal' students, the first group differing from the second only in that they undertook a small number of units in Year 10 (hence their identification as tasters/early starters). Beyond these two traditional approaches, the authority identified 67 different enrolment patterns of the many students who did *not* engage in this way, represented in the next eight lines. The final line indicates the numbers and completion rates of students whose 59 different enrolment patterns were too varied and little populated to include separately, probably the most interesting and challenging analytical data in the entire table.

Table 13.1 2000 SACE commencers' enrolment (all South Australian students), 2000–03

Pattern	Student numbers by pattern	Percentage of students by pattern	2000	2001	2002	2003	% of each pattern completing
1	4,976	22.9	T/Es	FT	FT	0	93
2	4,737	21.8	FT	FT	0	0	93
3	1,608	7.4	T/Es	FT	PT	0	41
4	1,608	7.4	T/Es	0	0	0	0
5	1,412	6.5	T/Es	FT	0	0	2
6	1,152	5.3	FT	0	0	0	7
7	1,000	4.6	FT	PT	0	0	32
8	978	4.5	PT	0	0	0	0
9	978	4.5	T/Es	PT	0	0	0
10	261	1.2	T/Es	FT	PT	PT	56
59	3,021	13.9	N/S	N/S	N/S	N/S	57
Total	21,731	100					55

T/Es = tasters or early starters (students enrolled in less than 4 units)
FT = full-time students (enrolled in 10 SACE units or more)
PT = part-time students (enrolled in less than 10 SACE units and more than 4)
N/S = not specified (these 59 enrolment patterns not individually identified)
0 = no longer enrolled

Source: Ramsay, E. (2008): 'The "absent presence" of part-time senior secondary study: a research and policy challenge', *The Australian Educational Researcher*, 35(2): 37–54.

Table 13.1 shows that the students in the first two lines, undertaking their certificate full-time over two years in the 'traditional' mode, make up about half of the commencing and more than three-quarters of the completing students during this four-year period. Is this an indictment of part-time study, indicating that it is indeed a cul-de-sac to nowhere? Digging below the many complexities of this data we found that it contains an overstatement of full-time and an understatement of part-time students' completion rates, because full-time students who dropped out of study appear as part-time students who failed to complete, the rationale being that their load overall was less than a full-time one throughout the entire year.

And what do we learn about the focus of our research, the part-time students? It is clear that an astoundingly large proportion of the state's entire commencing cohort did *not* engage with their senior certificate in what is assumed to be the 'normal' way, that is, full-time over two years. Confusingly, it does not in fact follow that they were part-time students for any of the years of their engagement with senior secondary certificate studies, but only that they *did not conform* to the assumed normal pattern. Note that the students in lines 4, 5 and 6 did not in fact undertake part-time study in any of the years of the period represented. And the students in line 4 undertook a very small number of units (less than four) and then did not continue. Is this a 'pattern of engagement'? Or might these be mature-aged students undertaking some SACE units for a range of personal enrichment related reasons, with no intention of completion, or returners finding out whether study is a realistic proposition given their other commitments? We can also ask whether lines 5, 6 and 8 reflect attrition rather than patterns of part-time engagement.

Accepting these cautions about what the data represents, there remain three lines which may actually contain students engaging with their SACE for one or more years in a part-time mode (lines 3, 7 and 10). Remembering that even these patterns will contain full-time students who left school mid-year, and noting that these students may later return and complete, together these three part-time patterns represent around 27 per cent of the 2,000 commencing cohort and around 23 per cent of the students who had completed four years later. Other issues to be taken into account in the table arise from the disparity between the authority's data on load at Stage 2/Year 12 and schools', teachers' and indeed students' approach to this, as noted above, the impact of which is to under-count part-time students at Stage 1/Year 11. Further there is an increasing trend for students to undertake a mixed load, that is, a combination of Stage 1 and Stage 2 units in any one year which confounds all definitions as well as the previously (and widely assumed) simple chronological correlation between students' ages, year levels and stage of study.

Why part-time study?

The expectation that paid employment underlies the choice of going part-time was not endorsed by the many students in our study. Clearly, paid work is part of the reality of senior secondary student lives, but participation in paid work of itself does not account for the phenomenon of part-time study. Indeed, more part-time students reported *stress* and a *desire to reduce SACE workload* as reasons for choosing part-time study than paid work commitments. The reasons given by students for part-time included re-entry into school, poor health, juggling paid work, unpaid care and other responsibilities with study, and as a strategy to increase tertiary entrance scores.

Comparisons with full-timers in their cohort are interesting. Paid employment was undertaken by 61.2 per cent of part-timers compared to 48.7 per cent of full-time students. Caring responsibilities were also a stronger feature of those enrolled part-time, with 53.8 per cent needing to offer care compared to a still significant number of 43.7 per cent of full-timers. Participation in community activities was also strong among part-timers, with 50 per cent of them engaged compared to 32 per cent among full-timers, and 72.9 per cent of part-timers contributed unpaid work in the home or business, compared with 59.3 per cent of full-timers. What this suggests is a set of changes to the overall landscape of young people, with participation in multiple institutions a 'normal' part of life. Part-timeness in this sense reflects the increasing complexity of senior secondary students' lives, cross-sector engagements, participation in a range of learning sites and leading to negotiation of multiple identities other than 'student'. Significantly, 70 per cent of part-time respondents reported that they felt part-time study would help them complete; and 60 per cent reported they would recommend part-time study. Most tellingly, approximately 30 per cent indicated that without the option of part-time study they would simply not be at school.

How schools respond to part-time students

Interestingly, almost none of the schools we studied had a documented approach to part-time study, nor indeed did the educational authority. Rather, the fact that the certificate could be undertaken over a number of years seems to have allowed part-time engagement by default rather than by educational policy design or pedagogical intent. Doing education differently in this case has grown from the ground up, in response to pressures on students' lives.

We broadly characterized schools' approaches to part-time study as proactive or reactive, although the policy vacuum meant they were often mixed in practice. Proactive whole-of-school approaches tried to make part-time an effective, deliberate and positive option for students so that they could take responsibility for and manage their study load in conjunction with the other domains of their lives. Usually, this involved inventing new practices or modifying existing school routines such as timetables, support structures and communication. Reactive approaches often treated part-time as a strategy of last resort, in order to keep students at school in some form; these schools did not make significant and meaningful adjustments to school routines and processes. Although elements of the more proactive approach were evident in several case study schools, only one offered part-time as an option to all students. The rest worked into part-time through using individual 'case management' processes to rescue students at risk of not passing or of dropping out altogether, usually after all other approaches (such as vocational education and training – VET – or community studies) had failed. Indeed the strong correlation between large numbers of part-time students and attendance at an educationally disadvantaged school appears to reflect this use of part-time as a strategy of last resort.

In our early readings of the data, it would appear that there is higher completion by part-time students where schools proactively manage decision making and management of students' study load. In such schools, students sit down with key staff to examine their overall life commitments and what schooling/subjects can be accommodated, part-time study being one of the options available to manage their time and achieve successful study outcomes. The key here is that study is seen as part of their lives and managed in the context of other commitments and activities, with some schools and some particularly talented teacher-navigators building upon learning wherever and whenever it occurs. In one such school, the honour board contains as many part-time as full-time students, and part-time engagement is a normal and successful part of managing study within students' busy young lives. So students may juggle work on the family farm/business with other caring work and schooling; or may work on VET certificates in paid employment, care for a child and also undertake some SACE subjects. Some may return to school, through a specific open access college, through connection to a school which allows off-campus study, through specialist programmes such as those for young mums, or through carefully structured fractions which allow access to a wide range of subjects over time as required.

Even during the time of the study (2004–07), there was a growth in numbers of students engaged part-time and there were indications that the marginal status of part-time mode was changing to become more positive. 'Leafy green' middle-class suburban schools had been nervous that allowing part-time study might signal a lowering of standards, while disadvantaged schools were wary that the demands of employers might increase the numbers of part-time students, increasing the 'slide out the door'. Now, more recognize that part-time study can reduce student stress, widen subject options, increase satisfaction and engagement, and maximize final scores on the completion certificate. The lack of centralized policy prescription has allowed well-managed schools and creative teachers to experiment with proactive approaches to achieving successful educational outcomes for students with complex lives. On the other hand, the absence of guidance on educationally effective approaches to managing part-time study, and its underlying causes, means that most schools struggle with what part-time study means and how to deal with part-time students when their structures, culture and processes revolve around outmoded conceptions of the 'normal' full-time student.

Doing education differently?

Our study showed how important it is to challenge the assumption that being a 'student' is an adequate descriptor of young people's lives and identities. Yet schools' and system's operations – which currently assume school as the most important locus of young people's activities and engagement – fail to acknowledge the impact and relevance of the many wider spheres of engagement which make up their students' lives. A significant percentage of young people – possibly half the cohort – does not engage with their final years of school in a full-time, two-year, lock-step sequence. Yet school systems, policies, procedures and resources continue to reflect outmoded assumptions about 'normal' students which position schooling above and apart from the rest of young people's increasingly complex lives.

Are we now in a position to answer the opening question about whether part-time schooling is a pathway or a cul-de-sac? The answer is, of course, that it depends. In schools reflecting outdated notions of the normal senior secondary student, assuming that all learning and activity of any significance occurs at school, part-time is used as a deficit strategy of last resort to manage 'at risk' students with little likelihood of success. In such schools, reactions to students wishing to study part-time range along a continuum from active resistance to begrudging accommodation. But where schools have included part-time study within a proactive approach to achieving positive outcomes for students with complex lives, providing serious advice and support, and rearranging the business of 'schooling as usual', then student engagement and completion rates both appear higher.

Our study is only just completed and the data are not yet fully analysed.

However, we have shown that the existence of part-time and extended engagement distinctly interrupts the linear and chronological notion of school cohorts, and linear notions of transition 'pathways' for young people from student to adult lives. Rather, what we are seeing is a significant blurring of the boundaries of transitions, and participation by young people in a range of institutions and other settings which include schooling to greater or lesser extents. Effective organizational and pedagogical responses to this shift, at the systems level, need to be informed by the strategies of schools which have positive engagement and completion rates for students engaging with their secondary certificate study in one of the multitude of different patterns available to them other than the assumed norm. The staff in these schools have moved away from 'pedagogies of indifference' (Lingard, 2007) to more systematic approaches that take account of the diversity and complexity of young people's lives in educationally sound ways. It is still too early to identify the completion outcomes for the student cohorts in our study since students who undertake one or more years of part-time load take longer to complete. However, early findings suggest positive schooling outcomes, including improved engagement and likelihood of completion, from organizational and pedagogical approaches which acknowledge and respond positively to the other activities in students' lives. Nevertheless, there remains a mismatch and tension between these approaches and wider systemic processes and requirements, and indeed community assumptions, about schooling and school students, which need to be challenged and changed. If schools are to catch up with their students who are 'doing school differently', then systematic changes will be required which build on the works of innovative schools and their communities.

Discussion questions

1. If young people participate in so many different institutions, why is the main term we use for them 'students'?
2. What specific practices in schools with which you are familiar would need to change in order to make them more flexible to accommodate a wide range of forms of participation?
3. Do you think that allowing part-time or different patterns of school engagement in senior secondary years is justified? Does it just accept that young people ought to be treated more as adults anyway?

Further reading 📖

Australian National Schools Network (2008) Draft policy paper on an Intergenerational Youth Compact. Retrieved 6 November 2008 from http://www.ansn.edu.au/report_from_the_national_forum_intergenerational_compact_for_our_young_people

Ramsay, E. (2008) 'The "absent presence" of part-time senior secondary study: a research and policy challenge', *The Australian Educational Researcher*, 35(2): 37–54.

Teese, R. (2000) *Academic Success and Social Power: Examinations and Inequity.* Melbourne: Melbourne University Press.

Websites 🖱

Australian Council of State School Organisation (ACSSO): http://www.acsso.org.au/

Dusseldorp Skills Forum (Australia): http://www.dsf.org.au/

Freedom-in-education: Part-time and Flexi-Schooling (UK): http://www.freedom-in-education.co.uk/Parttime_school.htm

14 Doing place and time differently in practice

Kathleen Ferguson and Terri Seddon
(Case study 14.1)
Kylie Twyford and Stephen Crump
(Case study 14.2)
Katherine Hodgetts (Case study 14.3)

The third theme of 'place and time' demonstrates how the stereotypical image of schooling as taking place at set times in a dedicated school building can be challenged. Chapters 11, 12 and 13 have offered research-based discussions about changes to the timing and location of schooling to better suit a diverse range of young people. This chapter complements those discussions through three practical case studies that demonstrate how 'place and time' can be done differently in practice. These are closely connected to the chapters: Case study 14.1 (Chapter 11), Case study 14.2 (Chapter 12) and Case study 14.3 (Chapter 13).

Case study 14.1 Lifelong learning in a café

Kathleen Ferguson and Terri Seddon

The Western District Social Partnership was formed as part of a state government policy initiative in Victoria, Australia. It aimed to support young people in their transition from school to working life, with a particular emphasis on those who had fallen through the educational network, and were at risk of social disadvantage and isolation. One of its initiatives, in partnership with local council and other stakeholders, was a training café.

The café is located on the foreshore of a coastal town. Its curved balcony and big windows look across the inlet towards a steelworks and oil refinery (both subject to workforce reductions). The training café was developed by the

Continued

local council, in an attempt to revitalize the area's economy and offer skills training to young people in a region with above average unemployment. The café was established, with modest funding from the state government, to conduct a 15-week project with 30 participants. It now employs people of all ages (in line with the shire's casual employment guidelines). Most are under 25. They serve an average of 380 people per day. At any time there are approximately 20 training participants, both 'back and front of house'.

Most participants are sourced from long-term unemployed in the region. There are two Schools Based New Apprenticeship positions (kitchen operations) with one designated for intellectually or physically disabled participants. The café can accommodate up to 15 groups at a time, from skills employment networks, and students from the local technical and further education institute (TAFE) who seek training in a practical working environment, rather than an institutional setting. These students are completing training that leads to national VET qualifications in Food Handling and Hospitality, Bar Tending, Occupational Health and Safety, and Coffee Making. Some are enrolled in stand-alone training programmes; others complete the certificates towards the Victorian Certificate in Applied Learning – the state-accredited vocational high school certificate.

The six-month courses include a written component and an examination, which are facilitated by one of several accredited trainers who work in the café, along with four professional chefs. None of the students are directly involved in cooking. They make and serve coffee, prepare food and clean up. The menu and its assembly is the preserve of the chefs, who are not required to provide training to the participants and may be seen as guides to be observed. The trainers encourage learners' participation. Limited local transport makes participation difficult for some, but there is good demand for places and returnee participation is not encouraged. After the six months, trainees have their hours reduced or are 'let go'. The café is acknowledged as an outstanding success. Participants speak of being 'put on their feet'. One trainee noted,

You gain hands-on experience which is better than doing mostly theory at TAFE. While I've been here, I've learnt that you can't do it all by yourself, when you start, it's an I-thing. 'I want to do this …' and you soon realize, if you want it done quickly and well, you have to work as a team. Personal presentation is important. You learn that there are ways of dealing with people. Now, when I'm a customer in places like this, I can see what they're

Continued

Continued

doing, I can say, 'I know this'.

This learning space is a commercial kitchen. It highlights the way services leading to employment in the hospitality industry are the primary, tangible goal of training programmes. Yet the production and consumption of food provides a window on what is also being learned in these spaces.

The social practices of dealing with food codify social norms and relationships, establishing hierarchies, patterns of inclusion and exclusion, and boundaries across which transactions occur. The learning subject being formed in these cafés is marked by these discursive practices. Transactions are about food and the performance of service. The learners learn to perform the bonhomie, the emotional and symbolic work that distinguishes the servant from those who are served, those who eat in restaurants and those who work in them. Consumption frames the identities and behaviours of both learners who wait (at table) and those they serve as customers.

Both cafés offer credentialled vocational training. Yet the credential, and training on which its award is based, seems insignificant compared with other pastoral, emotional, rehabilitative and relational learning that is going on. The training relationship is not centred – with teacher as source, and learner as subaltern subject. Rather learning occurs through participating in the site alongside others, trainees, chefs and customers. The emphasis is more on learning to be, and be in relationship, than to know. It is realized through learning relationships that respect difference, that embody care.

While such learning is seductively soft compared with training imperatives that stress control and the attainment of pre-specified objectives, it also works against the affirmation of learning subjects as knowers with the capacity to exercise power based on their authority as knowers. They train to wait but not to design menus or to be chefs. The pastoral and performative dimensions complement each other, encouraging and disciplining learners towards the sort of service behaviours expected in consumer societies.

Learning spaces like cafés are seen to be particularly relevant to young people who are disengaged from school and address skill shortages in areas of economic transition. Yet the kinds of working lives being made available to these young learners at the café are different to those who work at the steelworks and oil refinery. In the industrial sector, strong unionization, set job tasks and duration persist to a large extent. Those who service the café and consumer society confront the other side of the dual labour market.

Continued

Continued

The cultural consequences of this dual labour market are contested. Some fear cultural disintegration, undercutting collective capacity for living shared lives. Yet, the café defines itself as an actor in creating a sense of local identity. Students perform this agenda, building community with the café clientele and, in turn, sustain a larger group, a community of consumers who visit the venue to be part of a social milieu as well as to eat. As participants in this consumer partnership they also learn, drawn perhaps to the rehabilitative experience of these cafés and the opportunity to learn how to consume, materially and socially. And what do they not learn? Does it matter that they learn to work, to live with others, and perform the restricted forms of citizenship on offer within lifelong learning regimes?

Case study 14.2 Interactive e-learning for vocational education and training and indigenous Australians

Kylie Twyford and Stephen Crump

The tyranny of distance is a source of educational marginalization for Australian young people in remote areas. The introduction of Interactive Distance e-Learning (IDeL, see Chapter 12) has seen 'School of the Air' extend in recent years from primary education, to provide access to post-compulsory vocational education through technical and further education (TAFE). Opening entirely new opportunities for young people in remote areas, this has been a novel experience for students and TAFE teachers alike. Although much is still being learnt about the best ways of providing TAFE courses through IDeL, this case study provides some insights in how satellite distance education can improve access to education, especially for indigenous people.

At the TAFE NSW Western Institute (WI) in western New South Wales (NSW), vocational education and training (VET) courses are being delivered by IDeL to both indigenous youth and adults in remote communities in NSW and non-indigenous adults at isolated homesteads. For the indigenous students to attend an extended range of face-to-face VET courses at a TAFE campus would require travel for three hours by car each way – needing a driving licence, access to a motor vehicle and disposable income for petrol and accommodation. This

Continued

Continued

geographic isolation is one barrier to VET for indigenous youth in remote areas.

To address a need for 'work ready' skills in these remote areas, WI offers a range of entry-level VET courses. Often the subject and scope of the courses are designed in consultation with the communities to provide VET relative to local needs and employment opportunities. One such course designed and delivered by IDeL in 2007 was an introductory course in Beauty Skills.

Indigenous students in two communities attended the course. In Community 1, 12 students attended the first Beauty Skills lesson, while in Community 2 three students attended. Non-indigenous students from isolated homesteads were also enrolled. In the first lesson the teacher explained that the course was to see if the students wanted to work in the industry and pursue further education in this field. In doing so the teacher stressed to the students the 'vocational' importance of the course rather than it being a 'recreational' course. The subsequent lesson at Community 1 saw a significant drop-out in students. At the conclusion of the course, no students from Community 1 completed, while all three from Community 2 did, as well as four 'homestead' students. However, even for those who did not complete the course, the experience of IDeL provided insights not only in possibilities for accessing vocational education but also in how to use computer and Internet technology – new and important vocational skills in themselves.

The most important difference between Communities 1 and 2 was the support provided by the local assistant in the community, employed to facilitate the students to participate in the live synchronous lessons. The role of the assistant was to recruit students, help with enrolment procedures, assist with the set up of the room and satellite system, encourage students to attend and generally help to ensure the smooth running of the class. The assistant forms a crucial bridge between the community and the TAFE teacher hundreds of kilometres away.

The assistant in Community 1 was technically capable to set up the IDeL technology but did not provide the social and educational support needed, as a teacher commented: 'He wasn't engaged with the content himself, so he would do other things and they were left to their own devices.' In contrast, the other local assistant would not only get the classroom ready, but also encourage their attendance. Although this assistant did not have any knowledge specific to the Beauty Skills course either, she motivated and supported the students.

Support from indigenous TAFE colleagues also assisted the teacher. She

Continued

Continued

acknowledged that when she first began working with indigenous students she did not consider cultural issues. She explains what she learnt from a colleague who sat in on her first lesson:

> The first lesson I came and I sat here and I started to run the system. I remember her at the end, the students didn't say a lot, but at the end I looked at her and she said 'That's good'. And I said 'What do you mean?', and she said 'They've accepted you'. She said 'If they didn't accept you they wouldn't speak to you. So they were checking you out to see if you were someone that could be trusted, that they could respect, that you respected them, so that they could work with you'. And I didn't realize the whole sort of community interplay, you know the acceptance thing. It wasn't until then that I realized [teaching indigenous people is] very different from the norm. You have to gain their acceptance, their respect.

Respect from teachers is widely recognized as essential for engaging marginalized young people in education, but requires specific approaches not only with indigenous people, but within the constraints of the computer-mediated distance learning environment.

Establishing trust, respect and rapport as well as providing support for enrolment, learning and assessment are difficult through distance education, even with the ability for students to see the teacher through IDeL technology. The final suggestion from the teacher is to include face-to-face meetings at the start, in the middle and at the end:

> I want to have a situation where I meet everybody to start with and face-to-face we go through assessments, we go through setting out, structure of everything, we do all the enrolment forms [...]. And then twice a term we all come together so it's a lot easier then for me to do assessments, to know exactly where they are up to.

By offering classes via IDeL to remote indigenous communities TAFE is providing pathways to qualifications which could lead to employment that would otherwise not be available without indigenous youth having to leave their community and/or incur considerable expense in terms of travel costs and time. Though in this case study the results were mixed in the success of the Beauty Skills course, the case demonstrates the potential of satellite distance education such as IDeL to provide access to educational opportunities traditionally closed to indigenous youth in remote communities.

Case study 14.3 The school/life balance: part-time study and student well-being in a rural secondary school

Katherine Hodgetts

In South Australia, provision for the senior secondary school certificate (SACE) to be undertaken part-time has been available since the introduction of this credential in 1992. Yet most schools have used this option 'reactively', only allowing study load reductions in the case of struggling students, and those at risk of SACE failure. In this context, the proactive approach to part-time study adopted by Mt Gambier High School[1] (a rural school in the state's south east) stands out as particularly innovative. Mt Gambier has taken what was once understood as a 'failure prevention strategy' and made it a success – not by actively advocating part-time engagement, but by integrating study load reduction within a suite of strategies aimed at supporting student well-being.

Assistant Principal Toni Vorenas explains:

> We never set out to become 'the part-time study school'. It's really just that we saw our senior students struggling to juggle long hours of paid work alongside their study commitments and family responsibilities. They were feeling stressed and anxious and depressed – the balance wasn't there, and we needed to respond to that somehow.

Through the forum of the school's 'learning circles', students were asked to talk to staff about their responsibilities beyond the classroom. Teachers developed an understanding of the extent of their students' commitments – to paid and unpaid work, to apprenticeships and training, to caring for family members, to sport and to relationships. Poor academic performance was contextualized as students articulated their experience of feeling overwhelmed, and the mental and emotional consequences of their feelings of stress and pressure. Toni:

> It became pretty clear to us that when the going got tough for our students, and outside pressures mounted up, school was the first thing to drop. And we understood that. We knew that if our students wanted to go to university they'd have to move to the city – and that would cost money, so they'd need to work a lot while they were at school. And for students staying here

Continued

Continued

we knew that work experience was crucial. It wasn't reasonable to expect them to manage all that and a full load of subjects.

Based on this understanding, the school's leadership introduced a system for entry into senior secondary study that did not take for granted a full-time norm. Instead, students worked with teachers and subject counsellors to consider the 'pie' of their commitments, and the 'slice' they could realistically set aside for school. The focus was on sustainability and supporting well-being, and an increase in part-timeness was the result.

The mainstreaming of part-timeness into the culture of Mt Gambier High School brought with it some challenges. As part-time numbers increased, it became necessary to do away with school sign-in procedures, as students' patterns of attendance became increasingly complex. Eventually, all senior students were allowed to leave school grounds when they were not required for lessons. To respond to issues around duty of care, the school asked parents to sign indemnity forms to support the implementation of this policy. Students working part-time during the day meant that timetabling innovations were also needed. A number of subjects were offered outside the standard timetabling lines, and yet others were creatively rewritten into combined units requiring attendance only once a week. Communicating with part-time students also entailed creativity, and text messages and signboards increasingly came to stand in the place of face-to-face announcements.

Yet opening up part-timeness also brought numerous benefits. Importantly, staff identified improvement in students' well-being and results, also noting that their own understanding of students' lives enabled them to connect out-of-school learning to classroom activities in more supportive ways.

A particularly significant upshot of the school's part-time focus was the facilitation of dialogue with local employers. As the school supported and made space for students' part-time paid employment, it became all the more important to connect with the people responsible for those students in so many of their non-school hours. Toni:

It needed to be a partnership between us and the employers if we were going to support the students in a holistic way. We have the benefit of being a small town, so we got the major local employers together for a meeting here at school. Often the employers don't realize what goes on for these kids at school, and vice versa. So we had the conversation, and gave them

Continued

Continued

a calendar of the school's peak times in terms of assessment, exams, etcetera. And it meant we could get a sense of their peak times as well, and what that means for our students.

Observing the success of part-time study as an engagement option, the school recommends that other sites take up this strategy as part of a focus on well-being. In response to concerns that part-time study could result in students wasting or abusing their uncommitted time, Mt Gambier staff report that this has not been an issue at their school. New part-time students are initially monitored closely, but this does not need to be ongoing as students invariably settle into engagement patterns they have actively chosen and that they understand are designed to support their success. Likewise, staff explain that parental resistance to part-timeness has reduced as families have seen the well-being benefits associated with load reduction, and seen students grow in responsibility and self-discipline through making actively considered study choices.

As the names of part-time students have continually been evident on the end of year honour boards, both students and the school community have come to understand that this is not a deficit strategy, but one that can lead to a range of physical, mental and social benefits that are a platform for learning and success.

No one at our school sees part-time study as a failure, and that's a big part of why it seems to function well. We work with our students to ensure they make active decisions about their time, so that the study they're doing is sustainable and they can make it a success.

Note

1. Real names are used with permission of the school and participants.

15 Learning from indigenous education

Wanda Cassidy and Ann Chinnery

We have much to learn from Aboriginal and other indigenous peoples about doing school differently. In this chapter we focus on three features of indigenous education – relationship, respect and responsibility – and consider the implications of those features in light of the overarching themes of the book: identity, pedagogy, and place and time. The chapter:

- outlines key differences between traditional indigenous approaches to learning and the approaches that are currently dominant in mainstream schooling;

- suggests some ways in which the schooling experiences of historically marginalized youth can be improved; and

- explores the role of educational leaders in bringing about such change.

As we have seen in the preceding chapters, most current models of schooling are not structured to meet the needs of all students; and it is well documented that students from indigenous societies around the world are especially poorly served. Recent statistics show that in Canada, for example, only 47 per cent of Aboriginal students graduate from high school compared to 82 per cent of non-Aboriginal students (Mendelson, 2006).[1] In Australia, the completion rate is 43 per cent for indigenous students versus a general completion rate of 74 per cent (ABS, 2007). And in the USA, only 49 per cent of Native American students graduate compared to 70 per cent overall (Swanson, 2008). Unfortunately, too many students who drop out or are 'pushed out' (Fine, 1991) end up on social assistance or in minimum wage jobs and experience a reduced quality of life (Cassidy and Jackson, 2005).

From time to time there is a flurry of policy initiatives designed to assist the Aboriginal learner; yet, despite good intentions and significant funding allocated to such initiatives, Aboriginal youth still represent the group most likely to be failed by the system. Our language here is deliberate. Until recently Aboriginal students themselves were blamed for not succeeding in school. It was believed that they lacked the necessary intelligence, focus and problem-solving skills. Fortunately, this perspective is now largely recognized for what it is – uninformed, racist and representative of the dominant white culture – and it is now more widely recognized that the problem is not so much one of Aboriginal students failing school as it is of schools failing Aboriginal students.

In the following pages, we draw together some of the themes from the previous chapters under what might broadly be referred to as an indigenous education vision. Obviously we cannot do justice here to the richness and diversity of approaches undertaken around the world in the name of indigenous education, and we are well aware of the ethical dilemmas of white academics writing about indigenous education. But our hope here is to acknowledge and draw on indigenous approaches to education to explore how we might improve the experiences of marginalized (both Aboriginal and non-Aboriginal) youth in schools. Our discussion is rooted in the following beliefs taken from the British Columbia Ministry of Education's resource *Shared Learnings*:

1. Aboriginal cultures incorporate a distinctive sense of people's relationship with the natural world – a relationship characterized by a sense of connectedness, respect, and stewardship.
2. The wisdom and knowledge embedded within Aboriginal cultures continue to influence the world.
3. Aboriginal languages and traditions are living expressions of dynamic cultures.
4. Aboriginal peoples' spoken/written languages, communication protocols, and other forms of communication reflect distinctive world views.
5. Aboriginal artistic traditions are vital expressions of Aboriginal cultures.
6. The sophistication of traditional Aboriginal social, economic, and political systems continues to be a source of strength and direction for Aboriginal people.
7. Aboriginal people are continuing to define and affirm their individual and collective rights and freedoms. (1998: 8)

Briefly, indigenous education is based on a world view that sees everything in the natural world as interrelated parts of a larger whole; it is fundamentally about *relationship*. However, in the human and natural world, meaningful relationship cannot happen without *respect*; and respectful relationships are in turn characterized by a profound *responsibility*. Therefore we focus on these features of indigenous education – relationship, respect and responsibility – to help inform our understanding of the overarching themes of this book: identity, pedagogy, and place and time.

Relationship

In contrast to current models of schooling, which are based in western epistemologies that compartmentalize and de-contextualize knowledge, indigenous people have traditionally valued knowledge that comes through experience in and with the natural world. Particulars are seen only in relationship to the whole, and 'laws' are tested in relationship to survival on a daily basis (Barnhardt and Kawagley, 2003). Indigenous knowledge is thus holistic, stressing our relationship with all that is – with the physical, plant, animal and human realms – and the ways in which these realms interact to create unique knowledge or a higher knowledge in relationship with the spirit world.

According to Cajete (1994), traditional indigenous people are attuned in a profound way to the patterns and rhythms in nature, and he says that nothing in the contemporary modern educational experience comes close to fostering this sensitivity. We tend to neglect the affective domain in schools. We ask students what they think about something, but rarely ask how they feel. We ask them what they know, but give little credence to knowledge that integrates the mind, body, soul and spirit. According to Brown (2004), an Aboriginal educator, the affective domain must be given greater priority in school as this brings about healing and learning.

In indigenous approaches to education the learner is seen to be situated within a broad interconnected web of relationships. Indigenous education stresses experiential learning in natural settings involving meaningful tasks. Just as there is an assumed relationship between all that exists, indigenous approaches to education reflect a balance between the cognitive, affective, physical and spiritual dimensions of one's life. Indigenous education thus reflects an approach to learning that runs contrary to what we typically see practised in schools today, where competition is stressed over collaboration, in-school tasks are emphasized over community-based experiences, and success is measured by one's ability to memorize rather than one's growth as an integrated human being.

But in an attempt to make curriculum more relevant to Aboriginal students, well-meaning educators have also made mistakes. McDonough (1998: 486–7) relays a story told by Deyhle and Swisher (1997) about a teacher who tried to make connections with her Pomo Indian students by telling an ancestral story about Slug Woman. Several students responded with silence, while others were openly hostile. McDonough suggests that either the teacher misinterpreted the story as a genuine part of the students' identity, or students resented the fact that their teacher (an outsider) had appropriated a story without following proper cultural protocol. Whatever the reason, McDonough concludes that educators need to collaborate extensively with Aboriginal leaders and students before determining what should be taught, and that any curriculum should be approached with great sensitivity (1998: 486). Further, programmes designed to help Aboriginal students find success in the traditional school environment are doomed to failure unless the deeper issues of the institutional school culture are addressed (Harris, 2006; Stairs, 1994).

So how might these lessons help us to think differently about identity, pedagogy, and place and time? Educators who are committed to an indigenous approach to education must resist the temptation to ascribe certain characteristics, beliefs or values to their Aboriginal students. Neither should we assume that our Aboriginal students all have the same life experience. Some may come from communities where they have grown up hearing their traditional language spoken by elders, have been apprenticed into hunting, fishing or trapping, and have taken part in traditional ceremonies and rituals. Others may have lived in urban areas for several generations, and may have no connection to the land or particular traditions; but this does not make them any less authentic or any less Aboriginal. Affirming our students' identities means seeing them for who they truly are, in all the complexities that a relational sense of self implies.

Pedagogical strategies that affirm relationship emphasize observing and listening to each other rather than rewarding those who are always first to speak up in class. Teachers might invite a local Aboriginal Elder to speak about the meaning and value of sharing in indigenous cultures. Even pre-school aged children can learn about the importance of showing kindness and respect, about giving of themselves, giving what we most value, and the need to express gratitude for what we have received from others.

We also need to reframe our ideas about place and time in learning. Indigenous approaches to education allow for a natural flow of learning to occur over time, and the time frame is individualized for each learner. Learning a particular concept does not have to take place in a given week or a given grade level, as outlined in the prescribed curriculum. There is a careful attentiveness to what is innate and flows out from each individual, and this needs to be cultivated by the teacher in a variety of settings. This approach requires patience, an attribute that is in short supply in this fast-paced age of production and consumption. Part of this reframing of place and time is learning to question where we think knowledge resides. According to Battiste and Henderson (2000), each of us needs to recognize our innate knowledge and use it regularly, even daily. Further, Kwagley (1995) says that our personal cognitive maps are created and unfold as we interact with the natural and spiritual worlds and practice humility, tolerance, observation and humour.

Respect

While the term respect can be found in just about any mission or vision statement at the entrance of schools, what exactly do we mean by it? Does respect simply mean deference to authority? Or is it something more subtle? Reporting on a discussion about conducting research with Aboriginal communities, a recent issue of Charles Darwin University's *Newsroom* (2008) notes:

> While the importance of respect was acknowledged by everyone at the discussion, it was revealed that the Aboriginal concept of respect differed from non-Indigenous people's notions in fundamental ways … Associate Professor Helen Verran, of the University of Melbourne, who was in the audience, revealed her experiences of conducting research in remote communities … She spoke about how she discovered that learning and accepting the respect of the people of the community as a 'learner' was an important step in gaining respect and trust within Indigenous communities.

An indigenous understanding of respect thus requires a certain kind of humility in relation to what we know or can claim to know. Stairs (1994) also points out that if education is going to serve the needs of Aboriginal learners, it is critical that there be more than mere acknowledgement or accommodation of First Nations students. Rather, schools must be co-constructed together with Aboriginal communities in a spirit of deep respect (also see Case study 14.2 in Chapter 14). Respect needs to be shown for the validity of indigenous epistemologies and for integrating indigenous world views in the school curriculum, and in the way school principals and teachers reach out to develop authentic relationships with Aboriginal communities (Harris, 2006). As teachers, administrators and academics, we need to position ourselves as learners rather than knowers. Harris (2006) encourages us to listen to the quiet spaces between conversations, as this is where the spirit comes forth and fresh insights are found. It is only when true collaboration occurs that both the 'insiders' and the 'outsiders' are changed and something new and fresh is created (Stairs 1994: 1).

On a practical level, how might we begin to foster the capacity for respect in our classrooms in ways that support doing school differently? First, in Canada at least, where most public institutions are situated on traditional Aboriginal lands, it is important to acknowledge the traditional territory on which we are living and working. Teachers can also model and teach students about the importance of respect for elders as sources of knowledge. When elders are invited into the classroom, they are to be given the best seats, the opportunity to speak first, and to be listened to attentively. Just as we discussed above with regard to relationship, educating for respect requires a shift in our approach to pedagogy and place and time. It requires a move toward listening, patience and sharing:

> In traditional Aboriginal communities, Elders and grandparents were the teachers of the young children. The children were taught at a young age to listen. They were taught not to listen with just their ears, because anyone can do that, but to listen with their ears and their hearts. To learn how to listen was important for survival in the past and is still important for survival today. Elders taught young children to listen by sharing stories and legends that would keep the children's interest and attention. The stories would also have moral lessons that taught about sharing, respect, listening, and other values that were and still are important in Aboriginal communities. (British Columbia Ministry of Education, 1998: 133)

Respect comes through not just in our actions, but in our words and thoughts as well. As teachers and administrators, we need to listen too. We need to pay careful attention to the language we use to refer to indigenous peoples. We need to move away from deficit models where students' lack of success is attributed to a shortcoming on the part of the students themselves. And we need to talk openly about stereotyping – about the role of the media in constructing our perceptions of different groups of people, and about how those perceptions can creep into our assumptions about the indigenous students and families in our schools.

Responsibility

In indigenous approaches to education, even young children are given responsibilities in their family and community. In this section of the chapter, however, we focus primarily on the responsibilities of teachers and administrators who want to move towards a more indigenous vision of education in their schools. In considering this responsibility, it is important that educators see the school as a cultural creation where groups come together to negotiate meaning (Stairs, 1994), or as Giroux (1988) would say, the representation of lived experiences and practices forged between sometimes unequal groups. The school is not merely a building devoid of cultural meaning (historic and current), nor should its goal be to transmit the values and skills of the dominant culture. Schools, in other words, are sites of relationships not only between individuals, but also between different cultures, religions and world views; and the responsibilities these relationships entail run deep.

Indigenous conceptions of education challenge the educator to re-order school priorities to give more attention to building community and cultivating relationships in the human and natural worlds; providing more hands-on learning experiences that are meaningful and connected to life outside the classroom; incorporating indigenous traditions and the wisdom passed down from Elders; and valuing the learner as an integrated spiritual, emotional, physical and mental being. We suggest that educators carefully consider their own assumptions and beliefs about education and learning, and begin a process of self-reflection to determine whether their own perceptions are welcoming to indigenous perspectives, or whether they reinforce dominant western traditions, thus threatening indigenous students' success in school. Approaches that focus on interconnections, attentive listening, appreciation, respect and authenticity are valued in Aboriginal cultures, and need to be fostered if we are to move toward an indigenous vision of education.

But again, the challenge is how to realize this vision in our own schools and classrooms in light of the themes of identity, pedagogy, and place and time. One simple, but essential, task is to make sure that we know and observe the particular protocols of the Aboriginal peoples with whom we are working. As we saw in the example cited above by McDonough, the inappropriate use of an Aboriginal story in school may be worse than not using it at all. In Aboriginal communities many stories and dances belong to certain people, families or traditional groups, and it is very important that we obtain permission to use them before doing so. As teachers and educational leaders, we also need to take responsibility for learning about the history of indigenous peoples in our own area. In Canada and Australia, for example, it is vital that educators take responsibility for learning about the history of Aboriginal residential schooling and the tragic legacy it has wrought in Aboriginal communities.

As non-Aboriginal educators, taking responsibility for our identity also means taking responsibility for the unearned privileges that come our way simply by virtue of our skin colour – privileges that our indigenous students, families and colleagues do not share (McIntosh, 1990). In our own case, taking responsibility for our identity as white educators means asking ourselves what we will do to make schooling better for those students and families who have historically been marginalized by an education system designed for students and families like ours. By decentring white middle-class identities, we can begin to make space for Aboriginal identities and thereby support all of our students in gaining a greater sense of self. Much of what we have discussed above regarding relationship and respect also gives shape to our responsibilities as teachers and educational leaders, so let us close by offering some thoughts on the connection between an indigenous vision of education and the ethic of care discussed elsewhere in the book.

Tying it all together

As we mentioned at the beginning of this chapter, an indigenous vision of education focuses on relationship, and integrates the emotional and spiritual dimensions. This vision resonates with the burgeoning literature on the importance of an ethic of care in schools. Noddings, the most prominent writer in this area, has argued that the primary purpose of education should be 'to encourage the growth of competent, caring, loving and lovable people' (1992: xiv). For Noddings, teaching young people to care for other human beings, for self, for animals, plants and the physical environment, and for ideas, is far more important than the relentless striving for academic adequacy that is the current focus in schools. An indigenous education vision of co-creating a school environment where each person thrives – staff, students and their families, Aboriginal or non-Aboriginal – is a model that dovetails nicely with the ethic of care.

However, embracing an indigenous vision of education does not mean simply adding Aboriginal content to the existing curriculum. It means radically rethinking what we think and what we believe. It means inquiring deeply into our own values, beliefs, and assumptions about people from historically marginalized groups. It means questioning our own practices and taken-for-granted assumptions about how students learn and about what it means to be an educated person. It is hard work, and we will inevitably encounter resistance along the way, but we believe that the benefits to our students and their families and to society as a whole far outweigh the challenges: this is both the promise and the possibility of doing education differently for young people.

Discussion questions

1. An indigenous vision of education focuses on relationships and belonging. Where do you feel you belong, and what will you do to create a sense of belonging for the indigenous and other marginalized students in your classroom?
2. What challenges or difficulties do you think a school might face in moving from its current model to an indigenous approach?
3. Native American writer Thomas King says that epistemology can be thought of as the stories we tell ourselves about knowledge and what we take to be true. What do you think it means to know something? And how do you know that you know it?
4. What do you understand to be the core values in indigenous approaches to education? How might you begin to make those values real in the day-to-day life of your classroom and your school?

Further reading 📖

Cajete, G. (1994) *Look to the Mountain: An Ecology of Indigenous Education*. Durango, CO: Kivaki Press.

Christensen, L. (2000) *Reading, Writing, and Rising Up: Teaching about Social Justice and the Power of the Written Word*. Milwaukee, WI: Rethinking Schools.

King, T. (2003) *The Truth about Stories: A Native Narrative*. Toronto: House of Anansi Press.

Note

1. In this chapter, we use the term 'indigenous' in the global sense, to refer to original inhabitants on the land; and when we use the term 'Aboriginal', we are using it in its Canadian context, to refer to three designated groups of indigenous peoples – First Nations, Métis and Inuit.

References

Allen, M. and Ainley, P. (2007) *Education Make You Fick Innit? What's Gone Wrong in England's Schools, Colleges and Universities and How to Start Putting it Right*. London: Tufnell Press.

Anderson, A. (2008) 'Music lessons via satellite', paper presented to the Australian Computers in Education Conference, Canberra, 29 September.

Apple, M. (1987) *Is the New Technology Part of the Solution or Part of the Problem?* Canberra: Curriculum Development Centre.

Apple, M. (1993) *Official Knowledge: Democratic Education in a Conservative Age*. New York: Routledge.

Archer, L., Hollingsworth, S. and Halstall, A. (2007) '"University's not for me – I'm a Nike person": urban, working-class young people's negotiations of 'style', identity and educational engagement', *Sociology*, 41(2): 219–38.

Aron, L. (2006) *An Overview of Alternative Education*. Report to the US Department of Labor, Employment and Training Administration. Retrieved 13 September 2008 from http://www.urban.org/UploadedPDF/411283_alternative_education.pdf

Aron, L. and Zweig, J. (2003) *Educational Alternatives for Vulnerable Youth: Student Needs, Program Types, and Research Directions*. Washington, DC: Urban Institute.

Arthur, M., Inkson, K. and Pringle, J. (1999) *The New Careers – Individual Action and Economic Change*. London: Sage.

Atkinson, M., Johnson, A., Kinder, K. and Wilkin, A. (2004) *Good Practice in the Provision of Full-time Education for Excluded Pupils*. Slough: National Foundation for Educational Research.

Australian Bureau of Statistics (ABS) (2006) *2006 Census of Population and Housing*. Canberra: Australian Bureau of Statistics.

Australian Bureau of Statistics (ABS) (2007) *Schools Australia, 4221.0*. Canberra: Australian Bureau of Statistics.

Australian Bureau of Statistics (ABS) (2008) *Australian Social Trends 4102.0*. Canberra: Australian Bureau of Statistics.

Australian Industry Group and Dusseldorp Skills Forum (AIG)/(DSF) (2007) *It's crunch time. Raising youth engagement and attainment: a discussion paper*. Prepared by the Australian Industry Group and Dusseldorp Skills Forum. Sydney: DSF.

Ball, S. (2001) 'Labour, learning and the economy: A "policy sociology" perspective', in M. Fielding (ed.), *Taking Education Really Seriously: Four Years' Hard Labour*. London: Routledge Falmer.

Ball, S., Maguire, M. and Macrae, S. (2000) *Choice, Pathways and Transitions Post-16: New Youth, New Economies in the Global City*. London: Routledge Falmer.

Barnhardt, R. and Kawagley, O. (2003) 'Culture, chaos and complexity: catalysts for change in indigenous education', *Cultural Survival Quarterly*, 27(4): 59–64.

Barton, P. (2005) *One-third of a Nation: Rising Dropout Rates and Declining Opportunities*. Princeton, NJ: Educational Testing Service.

Battiste, M. and Henderson, J. (sa'ke'j) Youngblood (2000) *Protecting Indigenous Knowledge and Heritage: A Global Challenge*. Saskatoon: Purich.

Bauman, Z. (2001) *The Individualized Society*. Cambridge: Polity.

Beck, U. (1992) *Risk Society*. London: Sage.

Beck, U. and Beck-Gernsheim, E. (2002) *Individualization*. London: Sage.

Benard, B. (2004) 'How schools convey high expectation for kids', in B. Benard (ed.), *Turning the Corner: From Risk to Resilience*. Minneapolis, MN: National Resilience Resource Center.

Bernstein, B. (1977) 'Education cannot compensate for society', *New Society*, February: 344–7.

Bernstein, B. (2000) *Pedagogy, Symbolic Control, and Identity*. Lanham, MD: Rowman & Littlefield.

Bernstein, B. (2001) Video Conference with Basil Bernstein, in A. Morais, I. Neves, B. Davies and H. Daniels (eds), *Towards a Sociology of Pedagogy*. New York: Peter Lang.

Biesta, G. (2006) 'Interrupting hope', in D. Vokey (ed.), *Philosophy of Education Yearbook*. Urbana-Champaign, IL: Philosophy of Education Society. pp. 280–2.

Billett, S. Clemans, A. and Seddon, T. (2005) *Forming, Developing and Sustaining Social Partnerships*. Adelaide: National Centre for Vocational Education Research.

Billis, D. (2001) 'Tackling social exclusion: the contribution of voluntary organizations', in M. Harris and C. Rochester (eds), *Voluntary Organizations and Social Policy in Britain*. Basingstoke: Palgrave. pp. 37–48.

Bolton, G. (1986) *Gavin Bolton: Selected Writings*. New York: Longman.

Bourdieu, P. (1976) 'The school as a conservative force', in R. Dale, G. Esland and M. MacDonald (eds), *Schooling and Capitalism: A Reader*. London: Routledge & Kegan Paul.

Bourdieu, P. (1977) *Outline of a Theory of Practice*. Cambridge: Cambridge University Press.

Bourdieu, P. (1992) *The Logic of Practice*. Cambridge: Polity Press.

Bradley, H. and Devadason, R. (2008) 'Fractured transitions: young adults' pathways into contemporary labour markets', *Sociology*, 42(1): 119–36.

British Columbia Ministry of Education (1998) *Shared Learnings: Integrating BC Aboriginal Content K-10*. Retrieved 8 September 2008 from: http://www.bced.gov.bc.ca/abed/sharedlearning/SLsK-3.pdf

Brooks, R. (2006) 'Learning and work in the lives of young adults', *International Journal of Lifelong Education*, 25(3): 271–89.

Brown, L. (2004) 'Making the classroom a healthy place: the development of affective competency in aboriginal pedagogy'. Unpublished PhD Thesis, University of British Columbia.

Cajete, G. (1994) *Look to the Mountain: An Ecology of Indigenous Education*. Durango, CO: Kivaki Press.

Carnie, F. (2003) *Alternative Approaches to Education*. London: RoutledgeFalmer.

Cassidy, W. and Bates, A. (2005) '"Drop-outs" and "push-outs": finding hope at a school that actualizes the ethic of care', *American Journal of Education*, 112(1): 66–102.

Cassidy, W. and Jackson, M. (2005) 'The need for equality in education: an intersectionality examination of labelling and zero tolerance practices', *McGill Journal of Education*, 40(3): 445–66.

Centraal Bureau voor de Statistiek (CBS) (2007) *Statistisch Jaarboek 2007*. Voorburg/Heerlen: Centraal Bureau voor de Statistiek.

Charles Darwin University (2008) *Newsroom*. Retrieved 9 September 2008 from http://owl.cdu.edu.au/newsup/news/2008/Feb/E70B4895EF/

Colley, H., Boetzelen, P., Hoskins, B. and Parveva, T. (2007) *Social Inclusion for Young People: Breaking Down the Barriers*. Strasbourg: Council of Europe.

Collinson, V., Killeavy, M. and Stephenson, H. (2000) 'Hope as a factor in teachers' thinking and classroom practice', in C. Day and D. van Veen (eds), *Educational Research in Europe Yearbook 2000*. Leuven: Garant. pp. 21–35.

Considine, M. (2006) 'The power of partnership: states and solidarities in the global era', keynote address, Governments and Communities in Partnership conference, University of Melbourne. Retrieved 5 November 2008 from http://www.public-policy.unimelb.edu.au/conference06/presentations.html

Copenhagen Centre (1999) *New Partnerships for Social Responsibility*. Retrieved 21 March 2002 from http://www.copenhagencentre.org/main

Crump, S. (1995) 'Towards action and power: post-enlightenment pragmatism?', *Discourse: Studies in the Cultural Politics of Education*, 16(2): 203–17.

Crump, S. (1999) 'e-ducation: electronic, emotionless and efficient', *Journal of Education Policy*, 14(6): 631–7.

Crump, S. and Boylan, C. (2008) 'Interactive distance e-learning for isolated communities: finishing the jigsaw', keynote symposium for the Conference of the Society for the Provision of Education in Rural Australia, Melbourne, 28 August.

Crump, S. and Twyford, K. (2009) 'Opening their eyes: e-learning for rural and isolated communities in Australia', in K. Schafft (ed.), *Rural Education for the Twenty-first Century: Identity, Place and Community in a Globalizing World*. University Park, PA: Penn State University Press.

Crump, S., Tuovinen, J. and Simons, L. (2005) *Widely and Rapidly: A Report into Interactive Distance E-learning in New South Wales and the Northern Territory*. Sydney: University of Sydney.

Crump, S., Twyford, K. and Littler, M. (2008) 'Interactive Distance e-Learning for isolated communities: the policy footprint', keynote symposium for the Conference of the Society for the Provision of Education in Rural Australia, Melbourne, 28 August.

Cullingford, C. and Oliver, P. (2001) *The National Curriculum and its Effects*. Aldershot: Ashgate.

Dabbagh, N. (2005) 'Pedagogical models for e-learning: a theory based design framework', *International Journal for Technology in Teaching and Learning*, 1(1): 25–44.

De Bruijn, E., Overmaat, M., Glaude, M., Heemskerk, I., Leeman, Y., Roeleveld, J. and Venne, L. van de (2005) 'Krachtige leeromgevingen in het middelbaar beroepsonderwijs: vormgeving en effecten', *Pedagogische Studiën*, 82: 77–95.

Department for Children, Schools and Families (DCSF) (2008a) *Aiming high for young people: A ten year strategy for positive activities*. London: Department for Children, Schools and Families.

Department for Children, Schools and Families (DCSF) (2008b) *Raising expectation: Staying in education and training post-16*. London: Department for Children, Schools and Families.

Department of Communication, Information Technology and the Arts (DCITA) (2003) *National Communication Fund No 44 Interactive Distance eLearning Initiative Annual Report 2002/2003*. Canberra: Department of Communication, Information Technology and the Arts.

Department for Education and Skills (DfES) (2000) *Transforming Youth Work*. London: Department for Education and Skills.

Department for Education and Skills (DfES) (2004) *Every Child Matters: Change for Children*. London: Department for Education and Skills.

Department for Education and Skills (DfES) (2006) *Youth Matters: Next Steps*. London: Department for Education and Skills.

Department of the Environment Transport and the Regions (DETR) (2000) *Ward level indices of deprivation*. London: Department of the Environment Transport and the Regions.

Devlin, B. and Hutchinson, A. (2009) 'Interactive distance learning in "real time" for one student with hearing impairment: a case study', paper prepared for the ISFIRE conference, University of New England, Australia, 11–14 February.

Deyhle, D. and Swisher, K. (1997) 'Research in American Indian and Alaska native education: from assimilation to self-determination', *Review of Research in Education*, 22(1): 113–94.

DiMaggio, P.J. and Powell, W.W. (1983) 'The Iron Cage Revisited: Institutional Isomorphism and Collective Rationality in Organizational Fields', *American Sociological Review*, 48: 147–60.

Drop, B. and Volman, M. (2006) *De school is van ons. De visie van eigenwijze jongeren op voortgezet onderwijs*. Assen: Van Gorcum.

Dwyer, P. (1996) *Opting Out: Early School Leavers and the Degeneration of Youth Policy*. Melbourne: Youth Research Centre.

Edwards, R. and Nicoll, K. (2001) Researching the rhetoric of lifelong learning, *Journal of Education Policy*, 16: 103–12.

EigenWijs (2008a) 'De officiele EigenWijs website – Intake'. Retrieved 28 October 2008 from http://www.eigenwijs.org/index.php?id=intake

EigenWijs (2008b) 'De officiele EigenWijs website – Diversen'. Retrieved 28 October

2008 from http://www.eigenwijs.org/index.php?id=diversen

Elmore, R. (2006) 'Education leadership as the practice of improvement' UCEA Conference, Texas, 11 November. Retrieved 13 October 2008 from http://www.scottmcleod.net/podcasts

Ester, P., Vinken, H., Dun, L. van and Poppel, H. van (2003) *Arbeidswaarden, toekomst-beelden en loopbaanoriëntaties. Een pilot-study onder jonge Nederlanders.* Tilburg: Universiteit van Tilburg/OSA.

Falk, I. and Kilpatrick, S. (2000) 'What is social capital? A study of interaction in a rural community', *Sociologica Ruralis*, 40(1): 87–110.

Farrell, L. (2006) *Making Knowledge Common: Literacy and Knowledge at Work.* New York: Peter Lang.

Fenstermacher, G. and Soltis, J. (1998) *Approaches to Teaching.* 3rd edn. New York: Teachers College Press.

Ferguson, K. and Seddon, T. (2007) 'Decentred education', *Critical Studies in Education*, 48(1): 111–29.

Fielding, M. (ed.) (2001) *Taking Education Really Seriously: Four Years' Hard Labour.* London: RoutledgeFalmer.

Fine, M. (1991) *Framing Dropouts*. Albany, NY: State University of New York Press.

Finger, G. and Rotolo, C. (2001) 'Telephone teaching: towards constructivist teaching for rural and remote students', paper presented at the Australian Association for Research in Education annual conference, Fremantle. Retrieved 5 November 2008 from http://www.aare.edu.au/01pap/fin01158.htm

Foucault, M. (1977) 'Truth and power', in C. Gordon (ed.), *Power/Knowledge: Selected Interviews and Other Writings 1972–1977*. New York: Pantheon.

Foucault, M. (1988) 'Technologies of the self', in L.H. Martin, H. Gutman and P. Hutton (eds), *Technologies of the Self: A Seminar with Michel Foucault*. London: Tavistock.

Freire, P. (1974) *Education for Critical Consciousness*. London: Sheed and Ward.

Freire, P. (1994) *Pedagogy of Hope*. London: Continuum.

Freire, P. (2000) *Pedagogy of the Oppressed*. Tran. M. Bergman Ramos. 30th anniversary edition. New York: Continuum. (1st edn, 1970.)

Furlong, A. and Cartmel, F. (1997) *Young People and Social Change. Individualization and Risk in Late Modernity*. Buckingham: Open University Press.

Gale, T. and Densmore, K. (2000) *Just Schooling*. Buckingham: Open University Press.

Geijsel, F. and Meijers, F. (2005) 'Identity learning: the core process of educational change', *Educational Studies*, 31(4): 419–30.

Geurts, J. (2007) 'Het gaat om talentvol vakmanschap', *Gids voor Beroepsonderwijs en Volwasseneneducatie*. Deventer: Van Loghum.

Geurts, J. and Meijers, F. (2009) 'Vocational education in the Netherlands: in search of a new identity', in R. Maclean and D.N. Wilson (eds), *International Handbook of Education for the Changing World of Work*. New York: Springer.

Giddens, A. (1991) *Modernity and Self-identity: The Self and Society in the Late Modern Age*. London: Polity Press.

Giguere, S. (2006) 'Local governance for economic development: practice ahead of theory', keynote paper, Governments and Communities in Partnership conference, University of Melbourne, September. Retrieved 5 November 2008 from http://www.public-policy.unimelb.edu.au/conference06/presentations.html

Gilligan, C. (1982) *In a Different Voice: Psychological Theory and Women's Development.* Cambridge, MA: Harvard University Press.

Giroux, H. (1983) *Theory and Resistance in Education: A Pedagogy for the Opposition.* South Hadley, MA: Bergin & Garvey.

Giroux, H. (1988) *Teachers as Intellectuals: Toward a Critical Pedagogy of Learning.* Westport, CT: Bergin & Garvey.

Giroux, H. (2003) 'Utopian thinking under the sign of neoliberalism: towards a critical pedagogy of educated hope', *Democracy & Nature*, 9(1): 91–105.

Godfrey, J. (1987) *A Philosophy of Human Hope.* Dordrecht: Martinus Nijhoff.

Goleman, D. (1998) *Working with Emotional Intelligence.* New York: Bantam Books.

Goodlad, J. (1984) *A Place Called School.* New York: McGraw-Hill.

Goodyear, P. (2000) 'Environments for lifelong learning', in J. Spector and T. Anderson (eds), *Integrated and Holistic Perspectives on Learning in Instruction and Technology.* Dordecht: Kluwer. pp. 1–18.

Grace, G. (1994) 'Urban education and the culture of contentment', in N. Stromquist (ed.), *Education in Urban Areas: Cross-national Dimensions.* Westport, CT: Praeger. pp. 45–59.

Graham-Brown, S. (1996) *Education in the Developing World: Conflict and Crisis.* London: Longman.

Greene, M. (1991) 'Retrieving the language of compassion: the education professor in search of community', *Teachers College Record*, 92(4): 541–55.

Griffin, C. (2006) 'Representations of the young', in J. Roche, S. Tucker, R. Thomson and R. Flynn (eds), *Youth in Society.* London: Sage. pp. 10–18.

Halpin, D. (2003) *Hope and Education.* London: RoutledgeFalmer.

Harris, B. (2006) 'What can we learn from traditional aboriginal education?', *Canadian Journal of Native Education*, 29(1): 117–34.

Harris, M. and Rochester, C. (2001) *Voluntary Organizations and Social Policy in Britain.* Basingstoke: Palgrave.

Harvey, D. (2005) *A Brief History of Neoliberalism.* Oxford: Oxford University Press.

Hayes, D. (2005) 'Telling stories: sustaining whole school change in schools located in communities with deep needs', paper presented at the Australian Association for Research in Education annual conference, Sydney. Retrieved 5 November 2008 from http://www.aare.edu.au/05pap/alpha.htm#H

Hayton, A. (1999) *Tackling Disaffection and Social Exclusion.* London: Kogan Page.

Henderson, S., Holland, J., McGrellis, S., Sharpe, S. and Thomson, R. (2007) *Inventing Adulthoods: A Biographical Approach to Youth Transitions.* London: Sage.

Hochschild, A. (1983) *The Managed Heart: Commercialisation of Human Feelings.* Berkeley, CA: University of California Press.

Holdsworth, R. (2004) 'Good practice in learning alternatives', paper presented at the Learning Choices Expo, Sydney, 23 June.

Holt, J. (1995) *How Children Fail.* Rev. edn. Reading, MA: Perseus Books.

Human Rights and Equal Opportunity Commission (HREOC) (2000) *Bush Talks.* Sydney: Human Rights and Equal Opportunity Commission.

Institute for a Competitive Workforce (2008) *Leaders and Laggards: A State by State Report Card on Educational Effectiveness.* Institute for a Competitive Workforce.

Jessop, B. (1998) 'The rise of governance and the risks of failure', *International Social Science Journal*, 50(155): 29–45.

Johnston, K. and Hayes, D. (2008) '"This is as good as it gets": classroom lessons and learning in challenging circumstances', *Australian Journal of Language and Literacy*, 31(2): 109–27.

Jones, G. (2002) *The Youth Divide. Diverging Paths to Adulthood.* York: Joseph Rowntree Foundation. Retrieved 21 April 2008 from http://www.jrf.org.uk/

Kelly, P. (2006) 'The entrepreneurial self and "youth at-risk"', *Journal of Youth Studies*, 9(1): 17–32.

Kendall, J. (2003) *The Voluntary Sector: Comparative Perspectives in the UK.* London: Routledge.

Kohl, H. (1998) *The Discipline of Hope: Learning from a Lifetime of Teaching.* New York: Simon & Schuster.

Kolb, D. (1984) *Experiential Learning.* Englewood Cliffs, NJ: Prentice-Hall.

Korbijn, A. (2003) *Vernieuwing in productontwikkeling.* 's-Gravenhage: Stichting Toekomstbeeld der Techniek.

Kraus, K. and Sultana, R. (2008) 'Problematising "cross-cultural" collaboration', *Mediterranean Journal of Educational Studies*, 13(1): 59–83.

Krentz, J., Thurlow, M., Shyyan, V. and Scott, D. (2005) *Alternative Routes to the Standard Diploma.* Minneapolis, MN: University of Minnesota, National Center on Educational Outcomes.

Kruger, A. (1993) 'Local communities and urban regeneration: the contribution of community education', *Community Development*, 28(4): 342–54.

Kuijpers, M. and Scheerens, J. (2006) 'Career competences for the modern career', *Journal of Career Development*, 32(4): 303–19.

Kwagaley, O.A. (1995) *A Yupiaq World View: A Pathway to Ecology and Spirit.* Long Grove, ILL.: Waveland Press.

Lagemann, E. (1992) 'For the record: in praise of "the possibilist"', *Teachers College Record*, 94(2): 201–7.

Lange, C. and Sletten, S. (2002) *Alternative Education: A Brief History and Research Synthesis*, Project FORUM, Alexandria, VA: National Association of State Directors of Special Education.

Lave, J. and Wenger, E. (1991) *Situated Learning.* Cambridge: Cambridge University Press.

Law, B., Meijers, F. and Wijers, G. (2002) 'New perspectives on career and identity in the contemporary world', *British Journal of Guidance and Counseling*, 30(4): 431–49.

Lingard, B. (2007) 'Pedagogies of indifference', *International Journal of Inclusive Education*, 11(3): 245–66.

Local Learning and Employment Networks (LLEN) (2008) 'Connecting local groups to improve education, training and employment options for 15–19 year olds'. Retrieved 5 November 2008 from http//www.llen.vic.gov.au/

Maguire, M., Ball, S. and Macrae, S. (2001) 'Post-adolescence, dependence and the refusal of adulthood', *Discourse*, 22(2): 197–211.

Mandell, M. (2006) 'Do networks matter: the ideals and realities', keynote paper, Governments and Communities in Partnership conference, University of Melbourne. Retrieved 5 November 2008 from http://www.public-policy.unimelb.edu.au/conference06/presentations

Massey, D. (2005) *For Space*. London: Sage.

Matarasso, F. (1997) *Use or Ornament? The Social Impact of Participation in the Arts*. Stroud: Comedia.

Mayo, M. (1997) *Imagining Tomorrow: Adult Education for Transformation*. Leicester: NIACE.

McDonough, K. (1998) 'Can the liberal state support cultural identity schools?', *American Journal of Education*, 106(4): 463–99.

McGaw, B. (2006) 'Achieving quality and equity education', public lecture, University of South Australia. Retrieved 22 June 2008 from http://www.unisa.edu.au/hawke-centre/events/2006events/BarryMcGaw_presentation_Aug06.pdf

McInerney, P. (2007) 'From naive optimism to robust hope', *Asia Pacific Journal of Teacher Education*, 35(3): 257–72.

McIntosh, P. (1990) 'White privilege: unpacking the invisible knapsack', *Independent School*, 49(2): 31–5.

McLeod, J. and Yates, L. (2006) *Making Modern Lives*. Albany, NY: State University of New York Press.

McWilliam, E. (2002) 'Against Professional Development', *Journal of Educational Philosophy and Theory*, 34: 289–300.

Meijers, F. (1998) 'The development of a career identity', *International Journal for the Advancement of Counselling*, 20(3): 191–207.

Meijers, F. (2003) *Leren in de praktijk. Een onderzoek naar de mogelijkheden tot beroepsvorming*. Zoetermeer: Colo.

Meijers, F. (2008) 'Mentoring in Dutch vocational education: an unfulfilled promise', *British Journal of Guidance and Counselling*, 36(3): 237–56.

Meijers, F. and Wardekker, W. (2002) 'Career learning in a changing world: the role of emotions', *International Journal for the Advancement of Counselling*, 24(3): 149–67.

Meijers, F. and Wesselingh, A. (1999) 'Career identity, education and new ways of learning', *International Journal of Contemporary Sociology*, 32(2): 229–51.

Meijers, F., Kuijpers, M. and Bakker, J. (2006) Over leerloopbanen en loopbaanleren. Driebergen: Het Platform BeroepsOnderwijs.

Melucci, A. (1996) *The Playing Self: Person and Meaning in a Planetary Society.* Cambridge: Cambridge University Press.

Melucci, A. (1998) 'Inner time and social time in a world of uncertainty', *Time and Society*, 7(2): 179–91.

Mendelson, M. (2006) *Aboriginal People and Postsecondary Education in Canada.* Ottawa: Caledon Institute of Public Policy.

Milbourne, L. (2002) 'Unspoken exclusion: experiences of continued marginalisation from education among "hard to reach" groups of adults and children', *British Journal of Sociology of Education*, 23(2): 287–305.

Milbourne, L. (2009) 'Remodelling the third sector: advancing collaboration or competition in community based initiatives?', *Journal of Social Policy*, 38(2) (in press).

Miles, S. (2003) 'The art of learning: empowerment through performing arts', in A. Blasco, W. McNeish and A. Walther (eds), *Young People and Contradictions of Inclusion.* Bristol: Policy Press. pp. 163–80.

Mittendorff, K., Jochems, W., Meijers, F. and Brok, P. den (2008) 'Differences and similarities in the use of the portfolio and personal development plan for career guidance in various vocational schools in the Netherlands', *Journal of Vocational Education and Training*, 60(1): 75–91.

Muncie, J. (2006) 'Youth justice: responsibilisation and rights', in J. Roche, S. Tucker, R. Thomson and R. Flynn (eds), *Youth in Society.* London: Sage. pp. 81–9.

Munn, P. and Lloyd, G. (2005) 'Exclusion and excluded pupils', *British Education Research Journal*, 31(2): 205–22.

National Commission on Excellence in Education (1983) *A Nation at Risk.* Washington, DC: US Department of Education.

National Governors' Association (NGA) Center for Best Practices (2001) *Setting High Academic Standards in Alternative Education.* Washington, DC: National Governors' Association.

Noddings, N. (1984) *Caring: A Feminine Approach to Ethics and Moral Education.* Berkeley, CA: University of California Press.

Noddings, N. (1992) *The Challenge to Care in Schools: An Alternative Approach to Education.* New York: Teachers College Press.

Noddings, N. (1995) *Philosophy of Education.* Boulder, CO: Westview Press.

Noddings, N. (2002) *Starting at Home: Care and Social Policy.* Berkeley, CA: University of California Press.

Norris, N. (2007) 'Raising the school leaving age', *Cambridge Journal of Education*, 37(4): 471–72.

O'Connor, P. (2006) 'Young people's constructions of the self', *Sociology*, 40(1): 107–24.

Office of the Third Sector (OTS) (2007) *The Future Role of the Third Sector in Social and Economic Regeneration.* London: Office of the Third Sector, Cabinet Office.

Organisation for Economic Co-operation and Development (OECD) (2007) *Education at a Glance.* Paris: OECD.

Post, D. (2006) 'A hope for hope', in D. Vokey (ed.), *Philosophy of Education Yearbook.*

Urbana-Champaign, IL: Philosophy of Education Society. pp. 271–9.

Power, S., Rees, G. and Taylor, C. (2005) 'New Labour and educational disadvantage: the limits of area based initiatives', *London Review of Education*, 3(2): 101–16.

Ramsay, E. (2005–06) 'Life-wide learning and part-time senior secondary study', *The International Journal of Learning*, (12)10: 277–85.

Rawls, J. (1971) *A Theory of Justice*. Cambridge, MA: Harvard Educational Press.

Raywid, M. (1994) 'Alternative schools: the state of the art', *Educational Leadership*, 52(1): 26–31.

Reay, D. and Wiliam, D. (1999) '"I'll be a nothing": structure, agency and the construction of identity through assessment', *British Educational Research Journal*, 25(3): 343–54.

Rhodes, R. (1996) 'The new governance: governing without government', *Political Studies*, 44(3): 652–67.

Roche, J., Tucker, S., Thomson, R. and Flynn, R. (eds) (2006) *Youth in Society: Contemporary Theory, Policy and Practice*. London: Sage.

Rorty, R. (1999) *Philosophy and Social Hope*. London: Penguin.

Rose, N. (1999) *Powers of Freedom: Reframing Political Thought*. Cambridge: Cambridge University Press.

Rosenthal, R. and Jacobson, L. (1968) *Pygmalion in the Classroom*. New York: Holt, Rinehart & Winston.

Ross, S. and Gray, J. (2005) 'Transitions and re-engagement through second-chance education', *Australian Educational Researcher*, 32(3): 103–40.

Russell, D. (1999) 'AERJ Response', *Australian Educational Research Journal*, 36(1): 101–6.

Sanders, M. (2007) 'My Rortyian hope', paper presented at the conference of the Society for the Advancement of American Philosophy, Columbia (SC), March.

Sarra, C. (2003) *Young and Black and Deadly: Strategies for Improving Outcomes for Indigenous Students*. Quality Teaching Series: 5. Canberra: Australian College of Educators.

Schelsky, H. (1961) *Schule und Erziehung in der industriellen Gesellschaft*. Wurzburg: Werkbund Verlag.

Seddon, T. (1995) 'Educational leadership and teachers' work', in J. Smyth (ed.), *Educational Leadership: Cultural, Critical, Political and Gendered Perspectives*. Adelaide: Flinders University.

Seddon, T. and Billett, S. (2004) *Social Partnerships in Vocational Education: Building Community Capacity*. Adelaide: National Centre for Vocational Education Research.

Seddon, T., Billett, S., Clemans, A., Ovens, C., Ferguson, K. and Fennessy, K. (2008) *Sustaining Effective Social Partnerships*. Adelaide: National Centre for Vocational Education Research.

Seddon, T., Fischer, J., Clemans, A. and Billett, S. (2002) *Evaluation of Local Learning and Employment Networks*. Melbourne: Department of Education and Training.

Sedgers, J., Johnson, J., Smyth, D. and Waite, V. (2005) 'Interactive distance learning',

International Journal of Instructional Technology and Distance Learning, 2(10): 8. Retrieved 8 September 2008 from http//itdl/journal/oct_05/article09.htm

Shade, P. (2006) 'Educating hopes', *Studies in Philosophy and Education*, 25(3): 191–225.

Shotton, J. (1993) *No Master High or Low*. Bristol: Libertarian Education.

Siemens, G. (2005) *Connectivism: Learning as Network-creation, Learning Circuits*. Retrieved 5 November 2008 from http://www.astd.org/LC/2005/1105_seimens.htm

Smith, P. (2004) *The Quiet Crisis: How Higher Education is Failing America*. Bolton, MA: Anker.

Smyth, J. and McInerney, P. (2007) *Teachers in the Middle: Reclaiming the Wasteland of the Adolescent Years of Schooling*. New York: Peter Lang.

Snyder, C. (2002) 'Hope theory', *Psychological Inquiry*, 13(4): 249–75.

Solomon, E. and Garside, R. (2008) *Ten Years of Labour's Youth Justice Reforms: An Independent Audit*. London: King's College. Retrieved 22 May 2008 from http://www.crimeandjustice.org.uk/pryouthjusticeaudit.html

Spierings, J. (1999) 'A crucial point in life', in Dusseldorp Skills Forum (ed.), *Australia's Young Adults: The Deepening Divide*. Sydney: DSF.

SSABSA (2006) 'Response to the SACE Review Panel'. Retrieved 6 November 2008 from http://www.ssabsa.sa.edu.au/docs/sace-q/finalsubmission.pdf

Stairs, A. (1994) 'Education as a cultural activity', *Canadian Journal of Education*, 19(2): 121.

Stake, R. (2000) 'Case studies', in N. Denzin and Y. Lincoln (eds), *Handbook of Qualitative Research*. Thousand Oaks, CA: Sage.

Stokes, H. (2003) *Engaging Young People in School Through the Arts*. Melbourne: Youth Research Centre.

Stokes, H. and Wyn, J. (2007) 'Young people's identities and making careers', *International Journal of Lifelong Education*, 26(5): 495–511.

Stokes, H., Wierenga, A. and Wyn, J. (2004) *Planning for the Future and Living Now: Young People's Perceptions of Career Education, VET, Enterprise Education and Part-time Work*. Melbourne: Youth Research Centre.

Swanson, C. (2008) *Cities in Crisis: A Special Analytic Report on High School Graduation*. Retrieved 10 May 2008 from http://www.americaspromise.org/uploadedFiles/AmericasPromiseAlliance/Dropout_Crisis/SWANSONCitiesInCrisis040108.pdf

Te Riele, K. (2006a) 'Youth "at risk": further marginalizing the marginalized?', *Journal of Education Policy*, 21(2): 129–45.

Te Riele, K. (2006b) 'Schooling practices for marginalized students – practice-with-hope', *International Journal of Inclusive Education*, 10(1): 59–74.

Tett, L., Crowther, J. and O'Hara, P. (2003) 'Collaborative partnerships in community education', *Journal of Education Policy*, 18(1): 37–51.

Thurow, L. (1999) *Building Wealth: The New Rules for Individuals, Companies and Nations in a Knowledge-based Economy*. New York: Harper Collins.

Tyack, D. and Cuban, L. (1995) *Tinkering toward Utopia: A Century of Public School Reform*. Cambridge, MA: Harvard University Press.

United States (US) Government Accountability Office (2007) *Higher Education Tuition Continues to Rise, but Patterns Vary by Institution Type, Enrolment, and Educational Expenditures*, GAO Report, House of Representatives. Retrieved 13 September 2008 from http://www.gao.gov/new.items/d08245.pdf

United States National Center for Education Statistics (US NCES) (2002) *Characteristics of the 100 largest public elementary and secondary school districts in the United States: 2000–01*. NCES 2002–351, Washington, DC: National Center for Education Statistics.

Van Dam, E., Meijers, F. and Hövels, B. (2007) *Met Metopia onderweg*. Nijmegen: Kenniscentrum Beroepsonderwijs-Arbeidsmarkt.

Van de Loo, R. (2001) 'Loopbaansturing: De centrale rol van interne en externe dialoog', in M. Kuijpers and B. van der Heijden (eds), *Loopbaanontwikkeling*. Alphen a/d Rijn: Samsom. pp. 30–47.

Van der Werff, G. (2005) *Leren in het Studiehuis: Consumeren, construeren of engageren?* Groningen: GION.

Van Maanen, J. (1977) *Organizational Careers*. New York: Wiley.

Vickers, M., Lamb, S. and Hinkley, J. (2003) *Student Workers in High School and Beyond*. LSAY report 30. Melbourne: ACER.

Waldorf, L. (2002) *The Professional Artist as Public School Educator*. Los Angeles: UCLA Graduate School of Education and Information Studies.

Wexler, P. (1992) *Becoming Somebody: Towards a Social Psychology of School*. London: Falmer.

White, R. and Wyn, J. (2008) *Youth and Society: Exploring the Social Dynamics of Youth Experience*. 2nd edn. Melbourne: Oxford University Press.

Willis, P. (1977) *Learning to Labour*. Farnborough: Saxon House.

Wotherspoon, T. and Schissel, B. (2001) 'The business of putting Canadian children and youth "at risk"', *Canadian Journal of Education*, 26(3): 321–39.

Wright, N. (1989) *Assessing Radical Education*. Milton Keynes: Open University Press.

Youdell, D. (2003) 'Identity traps or how black students fail', *British Journal of Sociology of Education*, 24(1): 3–20.

Youdell, D. (2006) *Impossible Bodies, Impossible Selves: Exclusions and Student Subjectivities*. Dordrecht: Springer.

Zijlstra, W. and Meijers, F. (2006) 'Hoe spannend is het hoger beroepsonderwijs?', *Tijdschrift voor Hoger Onderwijs & Management*, 13(2): 53–60.

Zourzani, M. (2002) *Hope: New Philosophies for Change*. Sydney: Pluto Press.

Index

Added to a page number 'f' denotes a figure and 't' denotes a table.